Build the bridge between your dreams and reality

dream big
DO BIGGER

Hanna Olivas & Adriana Luna Carlos
Along with 21 Inspiring Women Authors

ISBN: 979-8-9869367-8-9

Table of Contents

INTRODUCTION

She Rises Studios was created and inspired by the mother-daughter duo Hanna Olivas and Adriana Luna Carlos. In the middle of 2020, when the world was at one of its most vulnerable times, we saw the need to embrace women globally by offering inspirational quotes, blogs, and articles. Then, in March of 2021, we launched our very own Women's Empowerment Podcast: *She Rises Studios Podcast*.

It is now one of the most sought out Women based podcasts both nationally and internationally. You can find us on your favorite podcast platforms, such as Spotify, Google Podcasts, Apple Podcasts, IHeartRadio, and much more! We didn't stop there. Establishing a safe space for women has become an even deeper need. Due to a global pandemic, women lost their businesses, employment, homes, finances, spouses, and more.

We decided to form the She Rises Studios Community Facebook Group. An environment strictly for women about women. Our focus in this group is to educate and celebrate women globally. To meet them exactly where they are on their journey.

It's a group of Ordinary Women Doing EXTRAordinary Things.

As we continued to grow our network, we saw a need to help shape the minds and influences of women struggling with insecurities, doubts, fears, etc. From this, we created a global movement known as:

Dream Big Do Bigger

Dream Big Do Bigger Are you Dreaming BIG? Is that all you're doing?

Have you turned your dreams into actionable steps?

This book is all about accountability and turning your dreams into reality.

It's one thing to dream BIG, but another to do even BIGGER!

Inside this book you are provided strategic methods and guidance to truly create the life and business you want to lead and live.

We carefully and intentionally selected women experts from around the world to contribute to the Dream Big Do Bigger movement for women.

There is no perfect time to start but right now!

Going small is easy and boring, but doing BIGGER requires stepping out of your comfort zone, leaning into your feminine power, gaining knowledge, investing in yourself, and understanding the importance of never giving up on your dream.

By dreaming BIG and doing BIGGER, you are challenging yourself to drop all limiting beliefs, self sabotage, imposter syndrome and really focusing on what it takes to make the BIGGER steps!

The book's mantra is **"Dream Big Do Bigger"**

All chapters were authentically written and represent each author's real life experiences and adversities. It is our purpose and mission to educate, celebrate and elevate women to become an unstoppable women influencer in life and business.

It's never too late to make a positive impact.

Here are five powerful reasons why you should Dream Big and Do Bigger:

- So you can live life without regrets
- You will help inspire other along your journey
- It's where the magic happens
- Learn to have faith in yourself
- Dreaming BIG will help you find meaning and purpose in your life

Women who dream BIG are happier than women who settle for less in life and business.

She Rises Studios offers:

- She Rises Studios Publishing
- She Rises Studios Public Relations
- She Rises Studios Podcast
- She Rises Studios Magazine
- Becoming An Unstoppable Woman TV Show
- She Rises Studios Community
- She Rises Studios Academy
- Fenix TV

We won't stop encouraging women to be Unstoppable. This is just the beginning of our global movement.

She Rises, She Leads, She Lives...

With Love,
HANNA OLIVAS
ADRIANA LUNA CARLOS
SHE RISES STUDIOS
www.sherisesstudios.com

Hanna Olivas

Founder & CEO of She Rises Studios
Podcast & TV Host | Best Selling Author | Influential Speaker |
Blood Cancer Advocate | #BAUW Movement Creator

https://www.linkedin.com/company/she-rises-studios/
https://www.instagram.com/sherisesstudios
https://www.facebook.com/sherisesstudios
www.SheRisesStudios.com

Author, Speaker, and Founder. Hanna was born and raised in Las Vegas, Nevada, and has paved her way to becoming one of the most influential women of 2022. Hanna is the co-founder of She Rises Studios and the founder of the Brave & Beautiful Blood Cancer Foundation. Her journey started in 2017 when she was first diagnosed with Multiple Myeloma, an incurable blood cancer. Now more than ever, her focus is to empower other women to become leaders because The Future is Female. She is currently traveling and speaking publicly to women to educate them on entrepreneurship, leadership, and owning the female power within.

INSPIRE AND EMPOWER YOURSELF

By Hanna Olivas

Dream Big, Do Bigger. It sounds so cliché, right?

Not when you truly realize that you only have one life, not nine. You begin to make your dreams and goals a priority, not an option. Every thought and action causes a reaction, even when you are dreaming. So the real question is how to inspire and empower yourself to dream big and do bigger things in your life.

Allow me to take you on a journey to help answer these questions and get to the root of why so many of us never see our dreams come to fruition.

We are all born and die. Those are two things every single person can count on. It's the how and when that are different for each of us. We all have a limited time here on earth. So why waste even a single second living in fear, doubt, procrastination, or unhappiness? What can you do right now to change your perspective and outlook on life? First, you must make yourself a priority, from your health to your wealth. Do not ever take your health for granted, because in addition to only having one life, you only get one body, so handle it with care, prayer, and love. We must begin and end each day with positive and truthful intentions. You live your life on purpose. Those dreams in your heart are there for a reason, and it's your responsibility to find out how to make them happen and take even bigger actions to see them through.

Stay consistent in your personal journey. We can't expect to get the best results if we start, stop, start, and stop. The old saying "go big or go home" is so true. Many of us tend to forget that. When life takes us through different adventures, trials, and tribulations, that is when we truly begin to understand how valuable our time is. I believe most of us win or learn. There is no luck. Almost everything that happens is a direct reaction to our thoughts. So if our thoughts are negative, so are our actions. If our thoughts are positive, so are our actions. It's that simple. Our subconscious leads the way. So if we are dreaming about an amazing life and opportunities, we are inspiring and empowering ourselves subconsciously to make them a reality. It's your choice to choose one or the other, so choose wisely. How do you ask? What you watch, what you eat, your good or bad habits, who you associate with, what you listen to, etc. They all turn into thoughts, and thoughts turn into beliefs and actions. We can all have limitless possibilities. Most fail because none of us like the growing pains or the unknown. We like security and safety. It's just human nature and our brains' way of protecting us. So if you truly want to grow, you must be willing to get uncomfortable and reprogram your mindset to believe that anything is possible.

As you read all the different chapters in this book, I hope you find what you are looking for and create the life you want to live, not run from.

Have that honest conversation with yourself and decide what you really want in this life.

Stay inspired and empowered.

With Love,
Hanna

CJ C Boyd

Queen By Design
CEO/Abundance Ambassador

https://www.linkedin.com/in/cj-c-boyd-525407254/
https://www.facebook.com/cj.boyd.50702
https://www.instagram.com/cjc_boyd/
https://msha.ke/cjboyd
https://queenbydesign.getlearnworlds.com

My name is Cathy Jo, but I go by CJ.

I was born and raised in a small rural town in Wisconsin.

As a young girl, I was content with knowing everyone by name and neighbors being family. I resigned myself to thinking I was destined to be just a tiny blip in the World and that I had peaked in High School.

As I became an adult, the small-town mentality actually became a detriment, and I set off to recreate myself in a new place.

As luck would have it, I moved around a lot in a short amount of time and desperately wanted to come HOME. The Universe delivered and I came back to my hometown when my Momma was diagnosed with Stage 4 lung cancer.

I now am on a mission to LIVE my life as a tribute to her because she was robbed of that opportunity.

HINDSIGHT IS 20/20 BUT TRUE EXPANSION REQUIRES VISION!

By CJ C Boyd

So many times we look at life in the rearview mirror, rehashing our past over and over. We attempt to make excuses and justify why our lives turned out the way they have. The problem with this mentality is that we continue to wallow in this same energy and NOTHING changes.

Reliving the past, fueling regrets, and continuing to measure the life we are currently living by the barometer of what we have always known suffocates our imagination and willingness to take a different path. It keeps us stuck in fear and repetitiveness. It isn't until we recognize the stagnation that our life has become, that we can decide to try new ideas, take different actions, and start to explore what a magical experience life can truly be.

I am a living, breathing example of what wallowing in the negativity of past actions, choices, and behavior can become. Having not truly embraced my past hurts, nor learned to heal myself from them, I went on to continue to put myself in similar situations without consciously realizing it. It wasn't until my entire life imploded that I realized I was the common denominator.

I was living my life on wash, rinse, repeat, choosing to continue to play small, to hide in my victimhood, and to not only accept but fulfill the role of "this is as good as it gets" and just be happy with what you have.

Sometimes life must literally strip you bare for you to recognize that there is more.

Once it landed for me that I had incredible power within, the ability to CHOOSE a different path for my life, and the duty to be a beacon of hope for others, was when I truly began to dream!

At first, I stepped away from being an employee and allowing someone else to command my every movement and assign my value. That got old right quick, and I decided that I didn't want to work for someone else the rest of my life. I dreamt about being my own boss, building a business of my own, and doing the things I wanted with MY time.

So, I decided to open a café. My love language, after all, was food. I ate to comfort myself and to feel loved and appreciated. When people raved about how delish my homemade biscuits and gravy, corned beef hash and eggs, and my signature "comfort bowl" were, I was ecstatic. I felt like I had FINALLY made my mark. I felt like I belonged and became successful.

I served my tiny little community that I grew up in. I gave back to the small town that had given me my start as a child, that had provided me with waitress jobs that helped me come out of my shell, with customer service jobs that honed my people skills, and built rapport and likeability because I was the 'girl next door' who everyone knew.

It was an amazing experience that provided me with the courage of knowing that I could do ANYTHING I put my mind to, could build a business from the ground up, with no financial backing nor bank loan, but merely on my own work ethic. It also taught me the importance of not having all my eggs in one basket, relying solely on myself, and the importance of automation and leverage to create true freedom.

The pandemic swooped in and that dream quickly came to a halt. I was forced to decide to either tread water until things opened back up or figure out a new way of life because bills still needed to be paid even though I had zero income coming in.

I Chose to Pivot!

While I absolutely LOVED the idea of the café and being a business owner, I realized that I couldn't continue that long-term without ruining my health. I also embraced the thought of "Wait a minute, if I can do this, I certainly am capable of so much more."

I admitted that I was still playing it "safe," relying on the skills that I had learned growing up, and was also limited by not only location reach, but also by my own small-town mentality that I had embraced as a kid that kept me selfishly thinking about ME.

IT WAS TIME TO GO BIG OR GO HOME!

So, I dove into the online space with a preconceived notion that I was on the cusp of something HUGE. What I quickly encountered was a space of useless noise, scammers, men looking to hook up, and an overall feeling of disdain and overwhelm.

I'm not going to lie; I was easy prey at first. I was desperate to make money, to find the golden ticket, to prove that I wasn't a failure, but most importantly, that I was capable. I started watching women who I resonated with, that seemed to be speaking my language, lived through similar life experiences but came out on the other side totally excited about life.

I kept doing the inner work: the gratitude, journaling, and visualization of the life I desired. I quickly became aware of the power these tools gave me. I literally could feel the weight of the world being lifted from my shoulders. I felt like I FINALLY had a path to follow, a blueprint that had worked for so many others, as well as the community that had my back—much like my hometown community, but on a MUCH larger scale.

Continuing to dive deep into my past mistakes allowed me to recognize the power of my creative ability, and once I tasted that power it was like fanning a flame inside myself. I was eager to expand, to grow, and to rip off the band-aid of all my excuses. I was able to experience the exhilaration once again that I felt when I owned my café. But it was deeper, more intense—like it had a mind of its own.

I ingested as much information as possible, attended every workshop and masterclass that I could get my hands on, and started to implement the tools I was learning. I was eager to pick up the pace and to land as many clients as possible, but most of all, I was eager to "hit the motherload."

The problem: I was doing this all from the energy of NEED, desperation, and scarcity. And guess what? The Universe delivered…and I was left feeling even more disgruntled and alone, because I was making it about ME. What could I get from it, how much money could I make, etc.

LIGHTBULB MOMENT

Someone I respected called me out. They told me I was being selfish, looking to serve myself, to make a name for myself, and to make money at others' expense. Man, did that change my course.

When I started being honest and taking radical responsibility for my bullshit was when things started to change drastically. I started sharing my story from a place of helping others, from the desire to show them that no matter what they have been through, there is a silver lining. I embraced more and more of the attitude I had in the café. That of serving others, being intentional about THEIR experience, and ensuring that they got delicious results.

I started to slowly realize the number of people I could reach, the impact I could have, the number of lives I could help change, and the quality of service I could provide. It was only then that I truly realized what it means to DREAM BIG, DO BIGGER!

We can impact on a grand scale when we make it about others, their desires, their hopes, dreams, and goals. When we meet people where they are and provide them with the tools and strategies that we know work, we can change the planet!

It is only when we serve others from a vision and mission of impact and from a conscious intention of guiding others to reach their highest potential, that we really live the life that we are meant for. We live on purpose, with a purpose, and to serve a purpose so much bigger than ourselves.

LIVING WITH VISION IS KEY TO CREATING A FUTURE FOR THE WORLD

Michele Meza

Luksi Coaching & Consulting, LLC/Certified Mindset
Coach and Branding Solutions Expert

www.linkedin.com/in/coachmicheled
https://www.facebook.com/luksiconsulting
https://www.instagram.com/coachmicheled/
www.luksiconsulting.com

For over 28 years, Michele Meza, also known as, Coach Michele D, has been a noteworthy leader in business and academia industries and is known for her work as the Branding Strategist at Luksi Coaching & Consulting; Michele has been featured in several well-known industry publications, books, and podcasts.

Coach Michele D has been honored with multiple recognitions, including a national leadership award "Native 40 under 40" for her contributions and expertise in business and Native American communities. She is formally trained in Organizational Leadership, holds a MBA, a Bachelor of Science degree in Entrepreneurship from Bacone College, and is extensively trained in strategic leadership. She holds certifications as a Business Process Manager, Green Belt in Lean Six Sigma, REBT Mindset Coach, and Emotional Intelligence Transformational Coach. Michele is involved in real estate and resides in Tulsa, Oklahoma. She's passionate about generational wealth and inspiring others to follow their dreams.

THE BULLETPROOF GOAL GETTER GAME PLAN

By Michele Meza

Introduction

In sports, strategy is critical to winning the game; it requires a game plan. Without the right strategy, the team doesn't stand a chance of winning the game. Additionally, the coach writes down the plays on a whiteboard or paper so the players will remember the plays and execute the actions needed to achieve the goal. The players can visualize how to execute the strategy during the game.

Studies reveal that 83% of the general population doesn't have goals, 14% have plans but not in writing, and only 3% have written goals. Research has proven that you are 42% more likely to achieve your goals if you write them down. There are many ways to write out your goals, which include whiteboards, on paper, on your mobile device, and by creating a vision board.

The dictionary defines bulletproof as safe from failure, without errors or shortcomings, and beyond criticism. When thinking intensely about the strategy connected to your heart's deepest desires, you must think about the big picture. Life throws curveballs at us through countless setbacks, negative thoughts or self-talk, life-altering obstacles, and bad seeds planted by naysayers. Most people allow these things to block or destroy their dreams completely. However, when we're goal getters, we don't allow those roadblocks to stop us. Instead, our strategies must be tight and bulletproof!

In this chapter, I'll share the bulletproof strategies I've created and executed, how to dream big, and how to set and implement big goals to achieve your wildest, massive dreams. Big goals inspire, guide, and deposit seeds of hope and confidence that nobody can take away from you. Dreaming big isn't for the weak; it requires dedication, perseverance, and execution. Don't only talk about it, be about it!

Get Your Mind Right

Before you develop your plan and create your goals, the first step in strategy development is mastering your mindset. Begin with conducting an inventory of your thought process. Ask yourself:

1. What do I say to myself on a daily basis?
2. What does my belief system look like?
3. What types of thoughts run through my mind throughout the day?
4. Do I have a lot of negative thoughts or positive thoughts?

One of the techniques I use is REBT (Rational Emotional Behavioral Therapy). REBT is an action-based approach focused on helping people work through irrational beliefs and teaching them how to manage their emotions, thoughts, and behaviors realistically. When people have irrational beliefs about themselves or their world, problems arise, resulting in negative thought patterns and mental distress. It not only creates a breeding ground for stressful situations or strained relationships but also causes people to live in fight or flight status, adversely affecting their health. Utilizing REBT allows people to recognize and change negative thought patterns to overcome psychological issues and mental distress. Based on the foundation of REBT, our cognitive perception, emotions, and behaviors are all connected. To understand the impact of situations we encounter throughout life, we must visit the beliefs we have about these experiences and the emotional response resulting from those beliefs.

I use the ABCDE model, which is the core concept of REBT. I love this model because it simply explains the reasoning behind our belief systems and thought patterns. It's also used in overcoming analysis paralysis and mental blocks. This technique breaks down that even though we might end up blaming external events for our unhappiness, our *interpretation* of those events actually activates our distress. ABCDE is:

Activating event (something happens in your environment)
Belief (your thoughts about the event)
Consequence (your emotional response to your belief)
Disputing (your thoughts and assumptions)
Effect (your preferred reaction and desired outcome)
Further Action (your next step)

The second technique I use with my clients is EI (Emotional Intelligence). EI is the ability to understand and manage your own emotions, recognize, and influence the emotions of others. According to the book *Emotional Intelligence 2.0*, EI is used to teach people how to deal with emotions creatively and beneficially employ our intelligence. People with higher EI are often people who have learned how to effectively manage their emotions and respond positively to the emotions of others.

The third technique I use is practicing daily affirmations, prayer, and meditation. I use these tools to keep me uplifted and aligned with my goals. Our environment plays a huge role in our ability to operate in a fully positive state of mind. As with wavelengths that occur in sounds, frequencies exist all around us. Those high or low frequencies directly affect our thoughts and actions. High-frequency people, what I call *goal getters*, operate in an energized state of well-being. Their aura is different. It's almost like an unseen magnetic force that draws you to them. The goal getters hold great conversations, inspire others, and deposit positivity into everyone around them. Their goals are big and their actions are bigger. They operate in an abundance mindset.

Manifesting 101

What is manifestation? Manifestation is the belief in a specific outcome you desire; it involves our thoughts and how those thoughts shape our reality versus planning and execution. It unites the current state with the future state as though it's already in existence.

How does it work? Manifestation requires discipline paired with actions. Decide on the frequency, which depends on the outcome's size and your desired timeline.

How do you practice it? For successful manifestation, you must be clear about what you want. Focus and fully commit to the desired outcome. Visualize what you want. Choose to think healthy, positive thoughts. Surround yourself with positive people and in a positive environment. Use manifesting techniques. For example, practice gratitude through journaling, meditation, prayer, and positive affirmations. Here's an example of a manifesting affirmation: I am blessed and abundantly living debt-free, happy, healthy, and whole.

Aligning Yourself with Your Goals

Dreaming big means setting goals aligning with yourself and what you want to achieve. You will receive your desired results when you and your goals are in harmony. Goal setting is not a one-time process; it's an ongoing thing. As you achieve various levels of success, your goals will change. A good place to start is creating your personal core values, which is how you view the ideal standards of behavior in yourself, your community, and your culture. You align your daily actions, beliefs, and life with your goals. Examples of personal core values are: Integrity, Family, Gratitude, Adaptability, Generosity, Courage, and Open-Mindedness.

Once you've identified your core values, it's time to set your goals. SMART goal setting is a method used to set achievable goals within a specific timeframe. SMART goals are:

Specific – Targeted areas of improvement

Measurable – Clear success metrics assigned to each goal

Achievable – Realistic breakdowns of each goal

Relevant – Fits within the scope of the project or desired outcome

Time-Bound – Realistic deadline

An example of a SMART goal is: I will increase the conversion rate of my website by 25% in quarter two, by optimizing the Call to Actions and changing the button size and location directly below the content. I will track goals in Google Analytics and review results monthly.

DNA Of a Goal Getter

Goal getters are people who continuously set challenging yet achievable goals and consistently accomplish their specific goals. Goal getters are equipped with specific tools. They persevere despite the challenges that arise while still meeting their goals. A goal getter's DNA or core makeup is discipline, nurture, and attitude. Here's how to apply specific actions and tools to the DNA of a goal getter:

Discipline – Applying the atomic habits technique, time blocking, and the MIT method (most important tasks)

Nurture – Applying the 80/20 rule to certain priorities or situations, building relationships with your team and clients, nurturing your actions tied to your goals, and following up (there's fortune in the follow-up)

Attitude – Practice having an attitude of gratitude, apply REBT to build a positive self-belief system, and affirming success through positive actions

Ready, Set, Execute!

Remember, my friend, Rome wasn't built in a day. Achieving success isn't mastered overnight. It takes intention and work, but the results are worth it! Your results are found in your daily activities. A solid strategy partnered with SMART goals will allow you to dream big and do bigger! My desire is that this chapter motivates you, inspires you, and ignites the passion inside of you. If you can dream it, you can achieve it. You can do anything you set your mind to.

If you have any questions or need guidance in achieving your dreams, please reach out to me. I'm here to help you make it happen!

What I do: www.luksiconsulting.com

Let's Stay Connected:
https://www.facebook.com/luksiconsulting
https://www.instagram.com/coachmicheled/
https://www.instagram.com/luksiconsulting/
https://www.linkedin.com/in/coachmicheled/

Lori Olson

The WNDX School of Mobile Apps
Founder & Lead Instructor

https://www.linkedin.com/in/loriolson/
https://www.facebook.com/wndx.lori.olson
https://www.instagram.com/wndxlori/
https://wndx.school/
https://wndx.com/

Lori is the founder and lead instructor at WNDX School of Mobile Apps, official training partner of DragonRuby. She is passionate about supporting a more diverse group of app developers create and launch successful mobile applications to address the needs of a more diverse global audience.

Lori has spent most of her career in Calgary, but now resides in her hometown of Lethbridge, on the traditional territories of the Blackfoot Confederacy (Siksika, Kainai, Piikani), the Tsuut'ina, the Îyâxe Nakoda Nations, the Métis Nation (Region 3), and all people who make their homes in the Treaty 7 region of Southern Alberta.

The best apps are created by people with lived experience, so Lori is on a mission to ensure the ideas from under-represented groups are given an opportunity to become the successful mobile apps needed by the women, the indigenous peoples, the seniors, the neuro-diverse, and the disabled.

YOU GOTTA HAVE A DREAM, BUT YOU GOTTA MAKE IT REAL

By Lori Olson

There are times in life when the future speaks to you and you just don't realise it. For me, that would have been on the streets of Lethbridge, Alberta—a dusty town on the western Canadian prairies—in the summer of 1983 when I was just a year out of high school. I was listening to the radio one sultry summer evening when the latest song from one of my favourite bands—Streetheart—came on. The first line of the lyrics would unwittingly portend my future:

You gotta have a dream but you gotta make it real

That simple line would become a guidepost for the most significant decisions of my career.

Can I Talk You Out of Your Dreams?

Unlike some kids, I didn't know exactly what I wanted to do in life. I loved math, chemistry, and physics in high school, but I also loved art. My aptitude tests all skewed heavily towards the sciences, but I was 'redirected'—to put it charitably—by my guidance councillors. This was fairly common for girls back then—they tried to steer us away from 'inappropriate' careers.

When the time to choose came, I wanted to go into geophysics, but I was told I should avoid that—perhaps because I wanted to study volcanoes. Regardless of the reason, that was bad advice, given most geophysics graduates in Alberta go into the oil patch or mining, which both pay pretty well. It was actually much worse than that, though. They dissuaded me because somehow it would be 'inappropriate' for a young woman—even if that young woman was a resource-industry geo-scientist—to work out in the field.

My second choice was astrophysics, looking for and studying extrasolar planets. I was promptly told, "You'll never get a job in that field." Little did I know NASA recruited out of the University of Calgary!

My third choice was pure math, and I was advised there were bad job prospects for that, too. Also bad advice, although I wouldn't learn of actuarial science for several years. Out of pure frustration, I randomly picked computer science because it was math-like, or so it was thought at the time. I was simply relieved to finally have chosen a field which my councillor could find no objections about.

(Not) The Smartest Kid in the Class

I enrolled in the University of Calgary Computer Science (CPSC) program with virtually no computer experience. This was the early 1980s, and those first-generation home computers were mostly marketed to young boys. This meant many of my male classmates already had computers and learned the BASIC programming language. These same guys often ended up being bored by the *Introduction to Programming* everyone was obliged to take.

Our household didn't have a home computer. Given I was starting with this built-in disadvantage, I was the opposite of bored! I had to work **really** hard to get up to speed and did fairly well as a result. As it turns out, I still use at least some of what I learned in that class today when trying to crack a coding challenge.

For the rest of my University career, the odds were seemingly stacked against me in various ways. Scheduling woes meant I could not always get the classes I wanted when I wanted them. There was a professor who had not come around to the idea of women in 'his' CPSC program, which caused further headaches and frustrations. It seemed if it wasn't one thing, it was another.

University equipped me to handle life situations where I was at a disadvantage. I learned when someone told me something could not be done, the best way to stand out from the crowd was to go ahead and prove them wrong and do it anyway.

Working for 'The Man'

Getting that first job as a university graduate is both exciting and scary. It's exciting, because I would finally have a full-time job, probably making more money than my parents ever had. Scary because it's a **full-time job,** and I had never had one of those before! What if I make a mistake? What if I hate it? What if I **get fired**?

However, I succeeded despite these concerns and stayed for almost a decade. There's not one piece of specific technical knowledge from my time with 'big oil' that I still use today. On the other hand, I did learn **tons** about personal and professional development that remained useful throughout my career as a software professional.

I could have been a 'lifer.' But when a round of downsizing came, I spotted a unique opportunity to chase after another of my life goals. I voluntarily took a package to pursue the exciting but uncertain world of entrepreneurship.

On My Own

My success or failure would now be entirely my own responsibility. I wouldn't have to share the credit with anybody. Then again, when failure came knocking, as it did from time-to-time, there was nobody else to answer the door but me.

Over these freelance and contract development years, I learned that if I wanted to advance my career, I needed a 'hook'—a unique expertise—to help me stand out from the crowd. In the early years, I tackled the challenge by becoming a member of *TeamB*, an exclusive, peer-invited group of software engineers who were expert users of development tools from a big software company at the time called Borland. *TeamB* provided expert advice to the rest of the community.

Consequently, I started speaking at local development group events, eventually leading to speaking and teaching workshops at conferences worldwide.

I had clients knocking on my door asking for my time, and I rarely had to look for work. There were bumps along the way, but overall I look back on this period with a lot of satisfaction. I worked on some interesting projects and made people happy with what I created for them.

Familiarity Breeds Contempt

Yet, I grew dissatisfied with just building software for others. All too frequently, the software I was hired to build was discarded or replaced. It seemed like these people paid me big bucks, but didn't know how to make that software succeed.

I eventually realised what I found most engaging was mentoring teams. I started creating workshops to help train other developers. I went all in and opened *The WNDX School* for teaching mobile application development. I created packaged, pre-recorded courses that built on what I had learned training in-house teams.

Having spent all my time and money creating content for my school, I was surprised to learn my years as a freelance and contract developer taught me **nothing at all** about how a business actually runs. Looking for a business mentor for myself, I ended up in Todd Herman's business coaching program *BaseCamp*.

Todd taught me that the *The WNDX School* needed **focus**. Instead of creating more and more courses, I needed just one thing to sell—a 'feature course.' This was mind-bending for me, but I did immediately have an idea: to teach developers about the **business** of creating mobile apps. And I worked hard on developing that concept.

When I proudly presented my results in the next group coaching call, Todd told me I was thinking too small. This was a course that I should be teaching to both business owners **and** entrepreneurs. Thus, *6 Pack*

Apps was born—along with the kernel of an idea which was a turning point in my career.

Discovering My Mission

There are two communities of learners with whom I had the good fortune to come into contact throughout my career:

First, there are the developers who simply wanted the hard skills required to be successful in their field. There are **lots** of coders who will be happy for the rest of their professional lives if they achieve this. That's great!

The second group was learning to code for a **very** different reason: they had a big idea they believed the world would just love if they could find it in the app store. Interestingly, a disproportionate number of these people were working from some significant disadvantages, such as sex, age, gender identity, or race. Based on my early university experience, I had real empathy for them.

That's when I decided to offer **two** versions of *6 Pack Apps:* one version for the first group, which was pretty close to what I had been doing all along, and a brand new one for the latter which was new territory for me.

Here's the secret sauce: the two courses are organised to produce graduates perfectly suited to the *other* community. For example, suppose you've attended *6 Pack Apps for Developers.* In that case, you will not only have some great, practical software skills but you will also have learned how to communicate and work in partnership with those who have graduated from *6 Pack Apps for Entrepreneurs.* If you've graduated from the latter, you'll be equipped to be a great client for those newly-minted mobile app developers.

I've learned there is no shortage of dreams that remain just that—ephemeral, illusive, and sadly never made real. *You gotta have a dream* **for sure**, but where I get my buzz, as Streetheart said so succinctly all those years ago, is when I help them *make it real.*

Beverley Lake

https://www.linkedin.com/in/beverley-lake-7740ab87/
https://www.facebook.com/beverley.heka
https://www.instagram.com/bevlake2019/
https://www.tiktok.com/@beverleylake1

Beverley Lake was born in Te Kuiti, New Zealand. She's a single mum of 4 boys and adores her grandchildren.

Growing up Beverley had frequent encounters with the spirit world, which scared her. She felt different, weird, and judged herself as she was never empowered to know how to work with the spirit world. And because of this lack of education, often used alcohol to suppress her thoughts, emotions, and feelings.

In 2020, Beverley was introduced to the tools of Access Consciousness, which changed everything.

Through using the tools she's learnt in attending many Access Consciousness classes she now acknowledges, embraces, and asks questions about what's hidden in the dark. She's turned towards the darkness that once scared her, and is cooperating with the spirit world again. She's in control, no longer afraid, and no longer needs alcohol to suppress her capacities.

Access Consciousness is about facilitating you to be your own expert, rather than relying on someone else's "truths", which is the key to accessing ease, joy, and glory in every area of your life.

Beverley has attended many classes and has a number of certifications including:

- Access Bars Practitioner and Facilitator
- Access Energetic Facelift Practitioner
- Access Body Processes Practitioner
- The Foundation
- Talk To The Entities Beginners Class.
- Enrolled, in Creative Therapy Course, 2023.

Beverley enjoys all Access Consciousness techniques and will continue upskilling.

GROWING UP DIFFERENT, MY FATHERS COFFIN

By Beverley Lake

Growing Up Different

I was born in 1968, and by the age of three and a half years old, I could see ghosts. I didn't know they were ghosts because they appeared like real people and not like a white sheet with no eyes, as portrayed in the old movies I was accustomed to watching.

The ghosts or spirits appeared in my dreams and sometimes, and when I was awake, they spoke to me. Sometimes they would just walk past, then they were gone. It was like there was an invisible portal (a child's imagination). I remember thinking, "We have a huge family, and they like to come visit." I did have a large family— sisters and two brothers. I'm the youngest of 12 siblings. My older siblings would sometimes get annoyed with me because they felt I was spoilt by our parents. I was a child who would keep to myself when my siblings were around, listening but not talking much. Although, there were times I would use being the youngest to my advantage to get what I wanted. My mother had nine brothers and three sisters; we never grew up with my dad's family. Most of my brothers and sisters had moved out of home, but they would often visit. My mother's brothers and sisters would also visit often, or we would go visit them.

Mum's Uncle

I recall my mum taking me and my three older siblings to the hospital to visit her sick uncle. He'd been in hospital for a long time. We walked into his room where he lay on a hospital bed. There was a hump in the middle of the bed where his feet were. I remember asking mum, "What's that there for?" My Mum whispered, "His legs are sore." Uncle could barely talk and was struggling to breathe. He looked at us four girls, and with pain in his eyes he smiled and said "Hello." I remember thinking, "He was walking and talking fine last night!"

The next day I was outside playing by myself when I noticed there were lots of little gold stars all over the ground. I started to pick them up and then ran inside and asked mum for a box to put my gold stars in. She gave me a small empty matchbox, so I ran back outside and picked up as many as I could fit in it. I went inside to show mum, and she gave me a strange look but said nothing. Later that day my mum got the news that her uncle had passed away. One of my sisters told me that Uncle had his leg amputated and that's why he was in heaven. That night when I took the box out of my drawer to play with the stars, they were gone. I remember thinking my sister had taken them, and I ran crying to mum. Mum then told me that there was never anything in the box, I was so upset. I thought she was only saying that so my sister wouldn't get in trouble with my dad. Looking back, I realize the stars were a gift from my Mum's Uncle. They were only left for me to enjoy for a short time. I still don't know why he left the gold stars.

I used to get very confused when we would go to funerals. I remember saying to my mum "I saw them last night, they said goodbye." Or sometimes I would say "Weren't they at our house last night?" My mum would acknowledge what I said but not discuss it. Sometimes I wouldn't say a word. Mum would just look at me and nod.

My Father's Coffin

Two months before my eleventh birthday I was walking slowly across a bridge into town with my head down when my sister called to me to hurry up. I looked toward her, and at the end of the bridge, I saw a coffin. Inside the coffin was my dad. Dad had been in an accident approximately two months before my vision. He was in the hospital in a coma, but he was still alive. I stood frozen while my sister yelled again to "Hurry up!" It felt like I was frozen for a very long time. Finally, I came back to this reality, and the coffin was gone. I never told my mum about the vision—I was scared. Was my dad going to die? I remember thinking, "If I don't talk about it, then it won't come true."

My dad suffered major life-threatening injuries to his whole body after he fell from a train while it was moving. I vaguely remember visiting him in the hospital, and he was hooked up to so many machines. I hated seeing him like that. I remember it being noisy, with lots of talking and people coming and going.

Tears from Heaven

There were 15 minutes left in my netball game when I said to my friend: "It's raining, but the sun's out." My friend said, "It's not raining!" I looked at her and said, "Then how come I'm getting wet?" I looked up to the sky and it was only showering on me. Moments later my two sisters were standing on the side of the court asking my coach if I could leave early because we needed to get to the hospital. That was the day my dad came home in a coffin.

Dad woke that day and spoke with mum and the nurses, but no sooner than he'd woke than he passed away. I believe the rain I felt that day on the netball court was my father's tears. They were warm and comforting. When I was told of my dad's passing, I didn't cry. When I saw him in the coffin at our house, I didn't cry, but I did say to mum: "That's what I saw at the end of the bridge last Friday!" She looked at me, took me into her arms, and we cried.

After my dad passed away, I remember hearing my mum talking. I asked who she was talking to, and she said "To Dad." I didn't see him, but she continued to have a conversation like she used to when he was alive. Yes, my mum had a gift: she could talk to spirits. Before my dad passed away, I used to hear her muttering and see her whispering. I never saw anyone there, and I assumed her behavior was due to old age.

Please Leave the Lights On

By the time I was 11, I hated seeing ghosts. Spirits were bad—they were a sign that someone was going to die.

I started to block the spirit world so they couldn't visit me, that way I wouldn't see any more loved ones die. As a teenager, I would judge myself harshly. I thought I was weird—could I really see spirits? During adolescence, I still had dreams/visions, and when I was old enough to drink alcohol I would drink lots to block the visions out… it never stopped them, but at least I had less. Well, really, I was just too drunk to remember.

In my late 20s and early 30s, I still had visions and dreams. It was harder to know what was real and who the spirits were. I talked with my sister a lot, telling her about my nightmares and out-of-body experiences. I felt trapped in a dark world. I thought I was dead. I was experiencing Astral Projections. I thought: please make this stop, I'm scared, will I die if I don't return to my body?

Aged 40 to 50 I was afraid of the dark and shadows, and I would ask to please leave the lights on.

Two years ago, I learnt a modality called Access Consciousness Bars that changed my life. I am an Access Consciousness Bars Practitioner and a qualified Facilitator. I've completed Talk to The Entities beginners' course and will further explore and open my knowledge back up to the spirit world so I can become the potent infinite being I've tried to block out for over 43 years. I have learnt Energetic Face Lift and selected Body Processes. I'm no longer scared of my ability; I know that I am stronger than the spirit world and I'm learning to work with them to have ease and joy. I'm no longer scared of the dark, and I no longer drink to forget.

Access Bars are 32 points on your head that, when gently touched, effortlessly and easily release the thoughts, ideas, beliefs, emotions, and considerations that stop us from creating a life we love.

Some benefits people have experienced include:

- Mental clarity
- Improved sleep
- Calmness and inner peace
- Reduced Stress, anxiety, and depression

Access Bars are used as a potent and pragmatic tool by families, wellness practitioners, schools, businesses, mental health professionals, athletes, veterans, artists, and many more.

It is practised in more than 100 countries around the world.

What would it take to unlock your true potential?

Dream Big, Do Bigger

Samantha Sheppard

Samantha Sheppard Consulting - Co-Founder of Mama Knows
Owner/Business and Marketing Consultant

https://www.linkedin.com/in/samantha-sheppard-b57649107/
https://www.facebook.com/samantha.lehmansheppard/
https://www.facebook.com/officialmamaknows
https://www.instagram.com/samantha.k.sheppard/
https://www.instagram.com/mama_knows_official/
www.samanthasheppardconsulting.com

Entrepreneur / Speaker / Mentor / Consultant / Mom extraordinaire

Samantha Sheppard is from Pennsylvania and thrives each day with Jesus and lots of coffee! She has 2 beautiful daughters that keep her super busy and alongside her husband, they have built a 7-figure business in the financial services industry. This has allowed her to experience all the ups and downs about building a business and the road to success that she is passionate about sharing with other entrepreneurs.

With a degree in marketing and over 20 years experience in the field, she is focused on helping other entrepreneurs reach their potential through business & marketing consulting. She also believes that each day should be spent on progress over perfection - especially on days that seem like a total hot mess!

Her favorite quote is from Eleanor Roosevelt "the future belongs to those who believe in the beauty of their dreams". In a world full of noise, STAND OUT!

BREAKING THROUGH THE BARRIERS

By Samantha Sheppard

It will always be there, but you have to refuse to let it stop you. What am I talking about? The barriers in life and business that will try and keep you standing still, or even moving backward. To be successful, you'll have to be part sass, part stubborn, and 100% relentless.

I have two daughters. My youngest is the definition of above and beyond. No matter the school project or how far the test is in the future, she is always studying, planning, and preparing. She doesn't want just a good grade by doing the bare minimum, she wants a grade she can be proud of. As adults, we can learn a lot from my daughter. To dream big and DO bigger, we have to go above and beyond the bare minimum and take action to make it happen.

To excel, we first have to know why we want to in the first place. Let's face it, to achieve any level of success you have to know that it's a grind. You have probably heard the question, "what is your why," right? Well, I have a challenge for you. Go deeper. Often the first answer we give is usually just the surface reason driven by something much deeper. Sometimes we don't realize our true 'why' until we force ourselves to reflect on its deeper purpose.

Let's try something: on a piece of paper, write the word WHY seven times along the left side going down the paper. Then, across from the first one, write your WHY for your goals. Then go deeper. Read your answer to the first line and then ask yourself, "but WHY is that important?" Then repeat that question to yourself and continue to do that until you get to the last WHY. The last one is usually the most honest and real answer to why you are doing what you are doing. We often give ourselves a surface answer to our 'why' and don't even realize it. However, in order to push past the barriers that will come when dreaming big and fighting towards our goals and dreams, you have to know why it matters to you so much. There will be many days where that answer, and solely that answer, will get you to push through.

Your purpose must capture your head and heart. The irony is that most people will want to negotiate the price for the prize. The bottom line is that you can't do that. The price comes **with** the prize. Maybe that means you sacrifice some time with your family for a little while so you can go to appointments or events to grow your prospect list. Perhaps that means you miss some birthday parties or events to help a client and solidify a relationship that will get you more referrals in the future. Whatever it takes is whatever it takes.

Sometimes the biggest barrier people avoid before it even happens is failure. I hate to break it to you, but failure and success are related. You can not have success without failure. Often the biggest lessons and growth periods come from the biggest failures. I am speaking from experience here! Every time something does not go your way or you fall flat on your face, you must get back up, brush yourself off and ask this: what can I learn from this? Every single failure is an opportunity to grow and learn. Most people do not see it because they choose to only focus on the negative of the failure, not the lessons that blossom from it. What we focus on is what expands. Focus on what you can learn from that experience and use it to move into your next stage. Your mindset will determine everything, so get comfortable with controlling your thinking because you are the only person with YOU 24/7.

Understand that on your path to success, those individuals who think they "have your best interest at heart" might very well be the ones who will be discouraging you the most. They will wonder why you miss all the family events, show up late, or leaving early. Maybe they will ask why you sometimes seem distracted by all the messages or calls you get from clients. Trust me, I get it. Getting some well-meaning advice from someone you care about in your life is hard, but you have to ask yourself: are they living the kind of life you're working so hard to build? I know that may sound harsh, but why do we take advice from people not living the kind of life we desire? We must stop letting other people rent space in our heads who are not leading the way for us and helping guide us toward our goals.

To break through the barriers, you have to be willing to hear NO a lot. You have to take the nos to say YES in the future. When my husband and I got our first business off the ground, we tag-teamed everything— taking care of the girls, running the office, attending family events, helping clients, and beyond. You name it, we tag-teamed it. So how did we decide who did what? On a piece of paper, we wrote a T-chart. One column said "home" and the other said "business." Then we wrote a complete (and long) list of everything that needed to get done in business and at home. Then we each chose the top five things we felt were the most important to get done and those became our priority for the next 6-12 months—adjusting as needed, of course.

Before becoming parents, we were both elbows deep in the business. As life changed, so did our roles. When our girls were little, my responsibilities were on the homefront, and my husband's were in the business. Having a business gave us the option to have me stay home, which was a priority for both of us before we even had children. As our children grew, I had more flexibility to become more involved back in the business. Now that they are young adolescents, I am able to have a more active role in our joint business, and I even launched my own marketing firm within the last year.

You see, the challenges you face in business (and in life) will always be moving targets. They will be different for years and years. To truly fight beyond the barriers you will face and go BIGGER, you have to pivot and adjust constantly. Once you feel like you have certain hurdles figured out, another one will pop its head above water and you'll have to redirect your energy and focus. It is part of the process. Too often we try to avoid the unavoidable, but we really need to embrace the change, adapt, and press on!

So, how did we keep dreaming big when we hit obstacle after obstacle? We kept stretching our vision and our circle of influence. To grow, you have to stretch, and the best way to do that is to surround yourself with people who force you to get out of your comfort zone. If we look at the nine people we spend our time with and their income and lifestyle, they can only teach us how to be the 10th just like them. To grow, you must constantly be thankful for where you are while hungry for more. This is how you push through to the next level.

A big barrier that my husband and I faced for many years was that we were extremely comfortable financially. It's weird to say that being financially comfortable is a barrier, right? We made a good income, had built some security in our business, had a nice home, and did not have to grind nearly as much as we had to in the first 10 years in our business.

However, comfort is the enemy of greatness.

We had to really have a gut check and think about our why in a larger sense. Were we okay with being complacent while having a comfortable lifestyle… OR did we feel that we were meant for more? When we had a truly honest conversation with ourselves, we felt it was selfish to only make enough income for us to be comfortable. We both knew that we had more in us to reach our true potential. By striving for that, it would allow us to grow our income to new heights in order to have the freedom of time and money to give back to our community at an even higher level. Giving back to our community was always part of our 'why,' but now it was more important than ever.

This entire book is about dreaming big and doing BIGGER. You will need to have a gut-check conversation with yourself and make a decision. If your goal is larger than what you currently have to give, then what needs to change to match that goal? You either have to push through the barriers to do bigger things or shrink those goals. Let's face it, no one wants to shrink their goals and dreams, so the answer is simple: Dream BIG and Do BIGGER!

Every single barrier you bust through is an opportunity for you to say YES in the future to someone or something that truly captures your head and your heart. Speaking from experience, you will never regret this journey. It is all worth it.

Sarah Thayer

Co-founder of Mama Knows

https://www.linkedin.com/in/sarah-thayer/
https://www.facebook.com/sarah.naomi.thayer/
https://www.instagram.com/sarah.naomi.thayer/

Sarah Thayer was born and raised in a self-employed family and grew up working in her family's businesses. She understands the joys and challenges of working for yourself. After college, she worked in human services, retail, and banking searching for her passion in life. She loved helping people, but never truly felt she was making a difference.

In 2015, Sarah and her husband, Owen, had their daughter and the pull of her heart to make more of a difference was stronger than ever. Evanora's amazing spirit inspires her every day and is the reason Sarah took a leap of faith to help families achieve their goals and dreams through financial empowerment.

She left her banking career of 10 years to start helping families and businesses with discovering how money works. Sarah is thankful every day for the changes she sees in her client's lives and the impact on their futures.

YOU'RE MORE THAN WHAT'S ON PAPER

By Sarah Thayer

Somehow as adults, we stop dreaming. Do you remember when you graduated high school and all your feelings about your future? Sure some were probably scary, but it was mostly the feeling of excitement. You were going to rule the world and change it for the better. Where did those feelings go? What happened that we forgot those? I hope to remind you to dream again.

My story probably isn't the most exciting or eventful, but it's mine and it led me to things I never thought I would achieve. The best part of my story is that I am still writing it, and I still have new dreams to dream and achieve.

It seems logical to start at the beginning, yet we aren't going to. I had a good childhood and grew up in a hardworking, entrepreneurial family. I am the oldest of three, and even though life wasn't perfect, it gave me the strength, wisdom, and motivation to pursue my future.

I want to share with you the good parts and a few of the not so good parts of my story, but these are some key moments that defined my life, goals, dreams, and so much more. In high school I was average, nothing special. I got good grades, played sports decently, was in the band, took dance classes, was a student trainer and manager, and even tried cheerleading. On paper, I was the typical high schooler trying to get into college. I enjoyed all of my activities and learned many things from them.

During my junior year, the Columbine shooting happened. This tragic incident sparked a dream in me to make a difference. With the help of my mom, I formed the idea to create an antiviolence club at my high school. I had some amazing friends who supported me, helped to develop interest, and took on leadership roles within the club. I spoke with my guidance counselor, who agreed to oversee and guide this new student activity. Pretty soon, we were a legitimate student organization. We even held a carnival-themed fundraiser, which was planned and run by the students. As a bonus, I was interviewed by a local newspaper! All of this is not something that would happen to a typical high school student, but it did.

The memories and experiences I gained from this moment in my life have stuck with me to this day. Having a dream, setting a goal, and seeing it accomplished creates a confidence boost you can't get through self-help books, attending seminars, or even flattering compliments. These things are great, but they are nothing compared to the confidence gained from having your dreams come true. I have always been a big dreamer, maybe even too big, and this pushed me to look past what others saw and focus on what I saw for myself.

Now you're probably thinking, starting a high school club isn't that big of a dream. But it was to me. I think you have to have super, crazy, awesome, big dreams, as well as ones that are pocket-sized. The pocket-sized dreams are the ones that , to me, matter the most. They are the ones that set you apart and make you dream more. They are the ones that pull at your heart strings and make your soul yearn to achieve them. They are the ones that make a difference in your life and others' lives.

After high school, I went to college as any typical young adult would. During the summer between my sophomore and junior year, there was a hiccup in plans and I didn't return for my junior year. I ended up working at the mall in a clothing store, and when you are barely old enough to be an adult, this is a dream job. I was offered a part-time manager position and loved it. Soon there was an opening for a full-time manager position, and this wasn't just any position. It was my dream job! At the time, the company I worked for sold men's and women's clothes separately at two different stores and they were testing the idea of creating one brand. Well, there was nothing special about me on paper, and in fact, I was probably the least qualified, but I wanted this new position. So I worked harder, covered extra shifts, built relationships with customers, and learned visual merchandising. So guess what? I got it! It wasn't easy, but I would do it again.

It was a pocket-sized dream I achieved. It led to so many wonderful memories, experiences, and friendships I could have never imagined. I learned so much and my confidence grew. If I didn't go for this dream, I wouldn't have had the courage to keep dreaming. After a few years, I decided I needed to return to school and couldn't do that working in the retail industry. So I designed a new dream: I was going to finish my bachelor's degree. I left retail to go into the banking industry. Again, I was probably the least qualified candidate on paper, but I used that to my advantage. I had learned customer service skills and how to resolve complaints, so I focused on that area during my interview and got the position. After working at the bank for a few months, I wanted to be an assistant manager. The first time I applied, I wasn't selected, but I didn't let that stop my dream. I became an assistant manager and then eventually a branch manager.

During my banking career, I returned to college and earned my degree. It wasn't easy, and I worked full-time managing a bank while going to school part-time in the evenings. Earning my bachelor's degree wasn't a pocket-sized dream; it was a big dream. Sometimes, when we have big dreams, they almost seem impossible to achieve. They seem even more impossible to accomplish when life happens. While working on my degree, I was fired. This was the worst timing, too. I had just bought my first house and hadn't even made my first mortgage payment. I am not going to lie, it hurt. Somehow though, my dream was big enough to keep me going. I could have easily gotten another position at another bank; in fact, I was offered one and turned it down. I decided to go for my dream. I enrolled in school full-time and worked part-time to cover my expenses.

Losing my job at the bank could have derailed my dream, but it was a blessing. I needed to complete an internship and wasn't sure how I was going to do it while working. Well, getting fired opened up my schedule to complete it and led to an opportunity for me to continue working after I finished my internship. Big dreams are never going to be easy to achieve. It's going to require setting goals and sticking to them. Sometimes you will want to quit and give up. You will question why you are doing this. I think if they were easy and we didn't grow along the way, we would all have the same dreams and life. There would be nothing that would set us apart and make us unique. The journey we take to get to our dreams shapes who we are and allows us to help others to achieve their dreams.

All of my big dreams, and even my pocket-sized dreams, lead me to keep dreaming. They gave me the confidence in myself to know I could achieve my goals. I don't think I would have had the courage to walk away from a full-time career, with a newborn to start a business without my dreams and struggles. On paper, I was a typical middle-class person. On paper, I was not qualified to start a business in an industry I was not an expert in, but I did. I have a dream to help people. I have a dream to help family businesses, just like the one I grew up in, achieve their financial dreams. I have a dream to help families create generational wealth and a healthy, strong money mindset. I have dreams I don't even know about yet.

You have dreams you don't even know about yet, too big and pocket-sized. Don't be afraid to dream about them, don't be afraid to achieve them, and don't be afraid of the struggles. If you're new to dreaming, start small. Close your eyes and think of something you want. Write it down and decide how you are going to get it. It can be a pocket-sized dream that leads to a whole big one that leads to a lot more. I am not an expert on dreams, setting goals, or achieving them. I just know if you dream it and work for it, eventually you will achieve it because you're more than what's on paper.

Dr Shelby Decker

Shelby Decker Enterprises
Business Strategy Consultant Coach Author Veteran Advocate

https://www.linkedin.com/in/shelbymdecker
https://www.facebook.com/shelbydeckerenterprises
https://www.instagram.com/dr.shelbydecker/
www.shelbydecker.com
www.shelbymdecker.com

Dr. Shelby Decker Is known for Turning Ideas into Profits specializing in business strategy, program development, and marketing. As a business expert, she creates strategic programs. Dr. Shelby Decker is a business strategy consultant and coach. Veteran advocate and contributor author. She uniquely creates initiatives to meet today's challenges for market gain. As a volunteer of a United Way of Broward County initiative, Mission United, Dr. Decker addresses veteran issues. Previous experience includes working with global corporations along with local and national non-profits. Dr. Shelby Decker attended Capella University for her Doctorate in Business Administration in the area of strategy and innovation. She earned her EMBA from the Jack Welch Management Institute, Strayer University. Her Bachelor of Science was gained at the Art Institute of Fort Lauderdale. She has a passion for helping others achieve their goals with inspiration, empowerment, and education for increased community contributions. Visit http://www.shelbydecker.com to learn more.

WHAT THE FUCK DO I DO NOW!?!

By Dr Shelby Decker

Oh, the Road that I Have Traveled and Led Me to Here

I climbed the corporate ladder. Work experiences included being a part of a large national department store's buyers' program, leading a consumer product company's division, being a top credit and collection representative, and managing product lines worth an estimated $14 million and $7 million. Then I moved on to acquiring a real estate portfolio that included 11 rental properties and creating from scratch a small business with an annual six-figure gross income. Wow! What a life I had! It was only when I completed my education journey with my doctorate that I fumbled. All the other times, I just picked up and quickly moved forward. Not this time. I got questions about what I was going to do with your doctorate. How was I going to build a career? What type of job did I want? Really? I am still trying to figure out where to go, where I should focus my attention, or what step to take next! I needed to focus on something! I needed to build a source(s) of income and definitely, needed to move on from my ten years of academic learning.

I did not have the luxury to take a vacation or have time to wander with the possibilities. I immediately focused my attention on the chaos of reigning in issues surrounding my parents' health. Each day was focused on money management, daily schedules, doctor appointments, estate cleaning, meeting with legal experts, and coordinating condo renovation projects. There was no time to focus on me. Still, daily, I questioned myself, "What the FUCK Do I Do NOW?!?"

The Year of Rebuilding

Those who read *Unleash Her* got a glimpse of the struggle that I went through to allow myself to embrace the new me. My accomplishments forced me to let go of the past and start again. This time I was not broke or alone. As mentioned in *Becoming an Unstoppable Woman Health and Wellness, I was burnt out as a caregiver* and started the healing process. I knew deep down I needed to take specific steps. I had the experience of leading others in different capacities. Now, it was time to grab the courage I needed to lead myself.

Me Leading Me

I started to walk the talk that I gave others. I continued to journal. The words written on those pages allowed me to explore my past, emotions, and thoughts. I added to my weekly routine activities like taking walks, Yoga, lunches with friends, and shutting the bedroom door for quiet time before bed. I treated myself to manicures, pedicures, and, yes, even a bra. That last one may not seem like an issue to you, but for me, it was a massive step of embracing my body after 14 months before going through my second double mastectomy. I became more productive by making lists, blocking my time, and combining tasks. Those habits remain. Next, I set deadlines. The targets were met, although several objectives slid into months later. I managed a condo renovation, my mother's healthcare, my father's life, and my own. It was in March of 2022 that I pivoted and allowed myself to be the center of my universe. That means I started putting boundaries. I started telling myself it was time for me to move forward. I need to build my life, my career, and my income. I had no idea how it would get done, but I had to walk in blind faith and remain calm during the storm. It was my choice to set the direction of my life and take responsibility for ending certain situations to a lesser urgency and make my "things" to a priority. In my ten-year academic journey, I shaped certain pieces of my dream life. It was always there and revealing itself more each year. The next step was vocalizing to others my desire to move on. I told them this had to be accomplished because I needed to concentrate on building myself. I started reaching out by networking, attending events, and agreeing to a leadership role with United Way of Broward County, Mission United.

The Universe Answered

With every step I took, opportunity presented itself. At a luncheon, I met a new friend helping me with my personal exercise goals and increased socialization. It also provided a chance to be in the newspaper. A friend's gathering gave me the chance of a casual conversation for leading a workshop. My social media prowl tipped me to writing my first book, *FiredUp!2,* and introduced me to She Rises Studios for the following three international best sellers and the upcoming two. I grabbed the challenges of improving my social media presence, selling my books, identifying my brand, and pushing myself to new levels of growth.

Why Stop?

I could have stopped after I gained my doctorate and just concentrated on being a caregiver to my family. I could have resorted to the comfort of working for someone else and building their business. That was not the answer. That would not allow me to be me. I unleashed myself and wanted to celebrate my hard work to get to this point. I had to go back and revisit my journals, vision boards, and class assignments to examine and analyze what was important to me. I looked for answers in those moments with scattered pieces of dreams before me. The solution came to me quickly. I have, in the past, grown others' businesses. It is time for me to start building a business for myself!

The past decade molded my desire to be my boss, have the freedom to arrange my schedule, and have multi-streams of income. I wanted to be a freelancer, a consultant, and a coach and grow others' potential— all on my terms! I have so much to give, share, and support others. Let's see. I am already part of the elite group. Harvard Business Review (August 2022) declared that only 2% of Americans have a Doctorate in Business Administration. It confirms that I am different and unique. So what is stopping me? I declared that I could not stop myself from fulfilling my dreams. I won't let anyone else and definitely won't allow myself to stand in my way!

Because I Can

Others question why I was a real estate investor. My reply was, "Because I Can!" Why am I doing this? Why not? I decided not only to take action to accomplish my dreams but to go beyond. I want to live the life that I have dreamed of—that life I envisioned on my vision boards. Life incorporates those ideas, blueprints, and discoveries in recent years.

Putting the Puzzle Pieces Together and Making It Happen

I loved to put puzzles together as a child. I developed a passion for strategy with Chinese checkers and board games in my preteens. My corporate life gave me a fondness for tracking numbers and aligning actions for small success. My academics opened the world of theory, deadlines, and research. It provided my preference for putting research and statistics (proof) into a strategic plan. I exercised specific steps to organize chaos for others, including my parents. I took those quiet times during those months of turmoil that had less drama to reflect and rediscover who I was now. My contributions to the books I was involved in allowed me to reflect, let go and embrace. It is time to take on a new responsibility and take charge of my life. I shifted and asked what I had yet to do. The voice emerged from within with a scream, "DO IT FOR YOURSELF BECAUSE YOU NOT ONLY DESERVE IT, BUT YOU ARE WORTH IT!" At that moment, I decided. I harvested the courage to take steps of action and unfold the possibilities.

Currently, I am designing online courses, developing product lines, consulting with small business owners, organizing workshops and retreats, and coordinating operations systems. My community impact has grown within the Veteran community and women empowerment groups. I regularly attend the Broward County Status of Women

Committee, which advises our county's commissioners on women's issues. My connections have increased both on social media and personally. I am a more significant influencer with transparency and vulnerability. Others trust me to guide them, and organizations welcome my input. Each day I look forward to the opportunities to cultivate relationships, including the relationship with myself. I remain focused each month, each week, and each day to act and move forward with my dreams. My new dreams from previous vision board creations are new goals, but I continue to grab presented opportunities to do what I did not dream possible. Crossing off one big dream allows you to move to accomplish a bigger dream!

Denise Oster

Doc Consulting, LLC
Precision Coach/Mentor

https://www.linkedin.com/in/denise-oster-dehn/
https://www.facebook.com/Deniseostercoach
https://www.instagram.com/deniseostercoach/
https://www.deniseoster.com/

Denise Oster is a magnetic force of spirited energy. Her tremendous ambition created a new dimension to her brilliance and beliefs. She values the magical vibration and unlimited potential we are born with. Her bold, sassy yet charismatic approach to life and exuberant personality is how she impacts others.

Denise has helped hundreds of clients expand their brilliance into unlimited success. Her experience and knowledge have eliminated self sabotaging beliefs and transformed into an inner flame that can't be dimmed. Her energy shifts your perspective and lights you on FIRE.

Denise's journey to excellence has been fueled by an unrelenting passion for empowering women to success. She holds a psychology and education degree, is a certified lifestyle coach, real estate agent, investor, and author. Her purpose originated from past obstacles of fears, low self-worth, infertility, miscarriages, divorce, single motherhood and uncertainty. She's about doing the heart work not the hard work.

GIVE FAITH A FIGHTING CHANCE

By Denise Oster

When something matters enough to you, it's worth pursuing. If it speaks to you and lights you up, then it's worth doing. We can find meaning in the pursuit of our dreams, but it won't happen by implementing something small. You know there is so much more in you, and you are tired of feeling stuck. You are tired of holding back, knowing you have big dreams, but you don't know HOW to make them a reality! Dwelling on the "How" impedes us from expanding to dream big and go bigger. It's not our job to figure out "the how." It's our job to have faith and move forward.

I notice most people get a quick hit of inspirational dopamine to take immediate action on their dreams, only to fall short or quit altogether. We quit because of all the excuses we fill our heads with. We lack faith in ourselves. We buy into our limited beliefs and bullshit. We are plagued by fear and may not even realize it—the fear of time, money, and success in ourselves. When we don't believe our actions will generate a reward, we are stopped dead in our tracks and may even change our dream to something smaller and safer. Keep it simple. It's not about what you are doing, it's about who you are being!

Humanize yourself, your dreams, and your faith. Believe in yourself to become the person that can move mountains. Discover the confidence in yourself that you are worthy of receiving these dreams. Be responsible for yourself, be vulnerable, and be willing to put your pride and ego aside. Master the fundamentals of your personal development before you bring it into your life and business. Become an expert at your inner game. Make a decision and choose yourself! If you are to dream big, it will require you to believe big. Dreams don't come true— you do! It all starts with giving faith a fighting chance.

Oh, how I wish I would have learned these lessons sooner in life. I think of the time, money, energy, and freedom I could have given myself. But there's no need to live in the past because this message presented itself at the perfect time. Messages and signs are given to us in mysterious ways. Ways which I previously ignored because I was not living my inner truth.

Years ago, while attending a conference, I was told I was "playing small." My immediate reaction was denial, confusion, and disbelief. I couldn't understand how I could attend a conference to better myself and my business yet still be seen as playing small. I was secretly pissed because I was so busy with work and couldn't possibly add anything more to my schedule. My days were a hot mess, jammed packed, and even pee breaks were penciled in, not guaranteed. To top it off, the other members in attendance were high-level people making obscene amounts of money that I couldn't even fathom. I didn't dare confess that I couldn't even afford the conference. I was stuck. I had no idea what was holding me back and keeping me playing small.

Weeks later, I received a follow-up call from the conference. I explained to the gentleman the valuable insights and takeaways during the week, but also my sheer frustration on not being able to fathom my pea-size brain mentality. I was determined to go bigger. He asked me if I had ever written a book. My initial response was, "NO" not even on my radar! "There you have it; there is an example of you playing small," he said! Then he proceeded to ask, "Why not?" I instantly fired off a zillion reasons, such as: Because this conference was for my investment business, not coaching; I've never thought about writing a book; I don't have a story; Nobody would want to read my book; I don't have valuable content that people would want; I don't know how to write a book; I don't feel good enough. After rattling off all of these excuses, I took a deep breath, a big sigh echoed through the phone, and tears started to stream down my face as I muttered into the phone, "Because

I don't believe in myself!"

At that moment, it hit me; I had no faith in myself. I was talking to someone who believed in me and saw my gifts and talents. He had complete confidence in me. He saw everything that I couldn't see! He saw what was holding me back and kept me playing small. He saw my lack of faith in myself. He allowed me to give myself permission to believe and see my gifts because I was too close to it. I was living in the middle of the forest and couldn't see a single tree. It was me that decided that I wasn't worthy or good enough to play bigger. He had faith in me that I was lacking. He had confidence in my abilities and my business. He was able to see it all. He showed me a different perspective that I never thought about because I didn't have faith.

The strongest message came through self-discovery that we women dismiss and bury our gifts because of our past. This can leave us not feeling safe or secure, like we are living in uncharted territory. When we are yearning for validation and approval from others, we quickly find ourselves stuck. We find it hard to move forward without someone else's permission. We question our worthiness, confidence, and enoughness. So why is it that we don't know why we are holding ourselves back, and it takes someone else to see our gifts? Because we don't have faith in ourselves. Who do you need permission from to play bigger?

Stop right here. Pull out a piece of paper and pen right now (do not type your answers out).

Answer these three questions:

What are your skills and talents?
List your talents and skills on the left side of the paper.

Who are the people that need these skills or talents?
Write your answers on the right side of the paper.

What do you need to do to get your skills and talents in front of these people?

List five actions/steps that you can take.

Whether you believe in yourself right now or not, this activity alone is an example of giving faith a fighting chance.

We can't dismiss the inner game. It is a proven method of mastering and overcoming your lack of faith in yourself and discovering your inner truths, which in layman's terms means "to our fullest potential." It's played within our mind and plays against obstacles like fear, self-doubt, limiting beliefs, focus, self-esteem, and self-sabotage. You are not alone. That's why it's the number one thing to address and conquer. You must understand the "INNER GAME" inside your head (self-talk). It's the relationship with yourself. It's how you perceive your outer world and the things around you. It's how you think, feel, react, and respond. Don't worry, we all have been handed some shitty hands in life—some more than others. The best part is that you are not broken, and the brain is a muscle, so we can restore and repair the old programming. We create stronger and better results when we consistently work on creating new habits and behaviors to rewire our thoughts. Let's face it, life and business can be overwhelming and leave us exhausted. Mastering the inner game will help you take success to the next level. If you genuinely want to play a bigger game in life and business, you need an amazing inner game. When you are feeling off, frustrated, angry, or insecure, chances are your self-talk is feeding you crap!

Girlfriend, here is what I did! I sat my ass down, got real with myself, and did a deep self-examination to gain clarity about my skills, talents, and gifts. I forgave myself for ignoring and not sharing my gifts with the world. I chose to make my dreams so big that people thought I was bat-shit crazy! Like delusional! I made a decision and lined myself up with it. Then I went all in on myself, changed my self-talk, discovered my inner truths, and leveled-up my inner game. I chose to have faith in myself and my ability to feel good. 28 days later, I submitted my manuscript to my publisher. I became an Amazon Best Selling Author! If I can do this, you can too! You don't need to hide who you are any longer. Make no apologies for the real and amazing person that you are. What is it costing you? Give your faith a fighting chance. NOW!

Erin Causer

Erin C Books

https://www.instagram.com/erincbooks
www.erincbooks.com
www.erincreative.art

My name is Erin, and I'm from Ontario, Canada. I'm first a disciple of Jesus, a wife to my wonderful husband, mother to my two children, and (now) author.

Years ago, I would never have envisioned myself writing a chapter for this incredible book. I have always dreamed of writing and received a lot of encouragement over the years to do so. The bridge from dreaming to doing remains a simple choice and an act of faith, even if that faith is as small as a mustard seed.

I finally decided to act on my seed-form dream of becoming a writer. Because of how my story has been written, I hope to inspire those who feel unseen or unheard, and encourage hearts to believe they have something valuable to share. Ultimately, I pray I somehow help women like me to overcome their own fears and "Dream Big, Do Bigger."

DON'T YOU EVER GIVE UP

By Erin Causer

Fear.

That is the number one mountain, setback, hiccup, cause of self-doubt, and the list goes on. So many of us are comfortable where we're at when there's this untapped creative potential to create something incredible with our lives and to build something that carries on to the next generation. As I crossed the bridge from fear (and settling for dreams as if they were an unreachable destination for me) to faith in myself and God, this simple but profoundly powerful step launched me into actionable steps toward actually achieving my dreams.

This is my story, and I trust an encouragement to fulfill your own dreams.

I graduated from the University of Ottawa in 2008 with an Honours BA in Psychology. I had no plans and no self-confidence, but I had a heart full of unfulfilled dreams. But how do I get there? One thing that brought me great encouragement was the writings of others in the form of books, autobiographies, biographies, non-fiction stories, and the bible. This season between my graduation from university(2008) and the year I decided to give my dreams one more chance (2021) was the longest, toughest road I think I will ever travel.

"The Road Less Traveled"
Robert Frost

Two roads diverged in a yellow wood,
And sorry I could not travel both
And be one traveler, long I stood
And looked down one as far as I could
To where it bent in the undergrowth;

Then took the other, as just as fair,
And having perhaps the better claim,
Because it was grassy and wanted wear;
Though as for that the passing there
Had worn them really about the same,

And both that morning equally lay
In leaves no step had trodden black.
Oh, I kept the first for another day!
Yet knowing how way leads on to way,
I doubted if I should ever come back.

I shall be telling this with a sigh
Somewhere ages and ages hence:
Two roads diverged in a wood, and I—
I took the one less traveled by,
And that has made all the difference.

Since that time, my professional life has been anything but straight and narrow. It has felt like ebbs and flows, valleys and mountaintops, and 180-degree turns and detours. Throughout this sometimes chaotic life journey, I have noticed a few things. Firstly, these experiences all created in my heart a deep longing for something more to be achieved in my life. I wanted great, not good, as we know the enemy of the great is good. I was living in this transitory state where nothing was seemingly permanent, except one thing: my faith in God. His goodness towards me and my unwavering belief that something great was about to happen if I just made it around the next turn were ever-present.

God has consistently encouraged me through friends, teachers, and professors at university that I had a writing style that was enjoyable to read. Writing always felt like natural work to me. Something I did in secret, something I loved but never dared to acknowledge, could actually turn into anything substantial.

Fast forward years and years, and I felt a little tug, a nudge if you will, from God to pick up my pen and get words on paper. But there was one thing stopping me.

Fear.

Like I said before, fear is a mighty opponent to achieving our dreams. If we can conquer self-doubt and fears, we are unstoppable. This is what I needed to do. Look fear right in the face and take one single, step toward my dream of writing.

But what if…

What if no one wants to read what I have to say? What if I'm actually a terrible writer? What if I'm a complete failure and sell zero books!?

It's time to kick down all 'what ifs' in your mind and exchange them for some…'what ifs.' Yep. You read that right.

What if what I say will touch so many lives and encourages so many hearts? What if there's actually some natural ability to express myself through the written word? What if I'm a complete success and outsell my goal targets? What if!

This is the direction I took my thinking and the first actual step towards crossing that bridge of fear to become a published author. As mentioned before, I am on my way to publishing my first-ever faith-based devotional (*Resonate: A 31 Day Maternity Leave Devotional*).

The first step was easy. I took stock of all the negative 'what ifs' I believed about myself and my dreams, and exchanged them for inspiring, unstoppable 'what ifs' and beliefs about myself and my dreams. I began to understand how powerful and effective it is to dream with God.

Second step? Do, or say SOMETHING. It's tough to steer a stopped car. So I began to inch forward and turn the wheel. As I started to do so, I knew I had something to write about. I knew that I had been given a voice, as have you, and that what I have to say matters. So I began to write, type, put thoughts down in words, and slug my way through what I was trying to express. The end result? My *Resonate: 31 Day Maternity Leave Devotional.*

Thirdly, there will be setbacks. I began penning down my first book three months postpartum. I was sick, had some postpartum complications, and healing took a long time. But I pressed on, and you should too. My setbacks throughout this year-long writing journey almost always came in the form of health struggles, whether it was me, my children, my husband, or a family member. Your setbacks to taking action steps toward your dreams may look completely different, but be certain they will come. And when they do, this is my advice for you: Keep going. Keep moving. Get back up and see this as an opportunity to rise.

Please, please, PLEASE do not give up on yourself, your loved ones, or your dreams. Ever. And that is the last thing I will write about that I learned. Before, when my professional life was obscure, and I was extremely replaceable, it was easy for me to quit and move on to the next thing. But your dreams deserve more than that. YOU deserve a life lived to the fullest, fulfilling your dreams and pursuing what you're passionate about. DON'T EVER GIVE UP.

"Don't Quit"
Edgar Albert Guest

When things go wrong, as they sometimes will,
When the road you're trudging seems all uphill,

When the funds are low and the debts are high,
And you want to smile, but you have to sigh,
When care is pressing you down a bit,
Rest, if you must, but don't you quit.

Life is queer with its twists and turns,
As every one of us sometimes learns,
And many a failure turns about,
When he might have won had he stuck it out;
Don't give up though the pace seems slow—
You may succeed with another blow.

Often the goal is nearer than,
It seems to a faint and faltering man,
Often the struggler has given up,
When he might have captured the victor's cup,
And he learned too late when the night slipped down,
How close he was to the golden crown.

Success is failure turned inside out—
The silver tint of the clouds of doubt,
And you never can tell how close you are,
It may be near when it seems so far,
So stick to the fight when you're hardest hit,
It's when things seem worst that you must not quit.

Annabelle Beckwith

Yara Journeys Ltd
Founder and Director

https://www.linkedin.com/in/annabellebeckwith/
https://www.facebook.com/annabelle.beckwith
https://www.instagram.com/annabellebeckwith/
www.yara-journeys.com
www.annabellebeckwith.com

Annabelle Beckwith has been a business consultant, coach, and trainer for over 20 years, working with entrepreneurs and business owners, SMEs and with Fortune 100 companies all over the world.

Her company - Yara Journeys Ltd - specializes in personal leadership development, team productivity, and business growth. Her primary focus is on working with people as human beings first - building individual clarity, confidence and capability - before working on their business goals and aspirations.

Her career has included work in daytime television production, in PR and marketing, and as Head of Development and Public Affairs at the Royal Scottish Academy of Music and Drama – varied roles and responsibilities that have given her a rare insight into human psychology in action.

More than that, her own journey and international lived experience have contributed to an approach which combines challenge with compassion, and wisdom with humor.

Her Amazon bestseller 'Get Your Peas In A Row – 5 key factors to propel your business forward', based on her extensive experiences, focuses on key principles for personal and entrepreneurial growth.

Annabelle is the proud mother of two millennials and lives in Scotland.

CROSSING THE BRIDGE: FROM DREAMING TO RESULTS

By Annabelle Beckwith

"Annabelle," he said. "You've just got to make yourself do it."

I'd always dreamt of becoming an author, but the thought of taking months to find an agent and then a publisher before even getting off the starting blocks made my heart sink every time I started researching the possibilities.

So I didn't start writing. Until one day trawling the internet forlornly for agents who might be interested in what I wanted to write about, a thought occurred to me: 'Whose permission do I actually need to succeed?"

My answer was inevitable: "No one's except my own."

My route to authorship changed in an instant. I didn't need an agent or a traditional publisher's 'permission' to write—I could self-publish.

The practicalities, though, were just the start. As I was writing *Get Your Peas In A Row – 5 Key Factors to Propel Your Business Forward*, I battled impostor syndrome daily. Despite over 20 years of working with business leaders and entrepreneurs internationally, I could NOT shake the deep-seated belief that I was a fraud, that my experience didn't count, that people already knew what I had to say, and that nobody would listen to me. And with these beliefs holding me back, I dithered and dawdled and procrastinated, all the while giving myself 'reasons' for doing so, and the book wasn't getting written.

Until one day, a good friend called me on my BS: "Annabelle," he said. "You've just got to make yourself do it."

In a nutshell, this is where dreams become a reality: not in the dreaming, not in the planning, but in the DOING. In the uncertain steps forward, the cautious exploration, the timid pushing through… in doing SOMEthing to move forward, regardless of fear or self-doubt.

It's the courage to start that's the biggest step.

Decisions, Decisions…

Imagine that you see a bridge before you: a long one where you can't see over to the other side, but you know what's there. Here in Scotland, we have a number of bridges that link islands to the mainland. They cross ancient castle moats and span major rivers and estuaries. Sometimes, it's foggy and you can't see to the middle of the bridge (San Francisco, anyone?!). There are three things that prompt you to cross:

- You know what's on the other side.
- You want to get there.
- That's where you want to be, instead of where you are now.

Where is it YOU want to go? What do YOU want to achieve? What's on the other side of the bridge for YOU?

The decision to cross starts here. I once heard Bob Proctor explain the origins of the word 'decision,' from the Latin meaning 'to cut off from.' Deciding to do something literally means cutting ourselves off from other possibilities.

We can only really do that if we make a committed decision to see it through, whatever it takes, not just one of those "I'll see how it goes and bale out if it gets uncomfortable" decisions.

Making a clear decision shifts your mindset from one of hesitation to one of purpose. Once I realized that my friend was right and I DID have to make myself write the book, regardless of my fears and self doubt, I set about putting things in place to help, like scheduling a proof reader, thereby giving myself a deadline to work to, and getting up early each morning to write a little bit and move forward step by step.

Once you've decided to cross the bridge, don't hesitate. Take your first step. Start. Waiting till you feel more confident about moving forward may hold you up: just stepping out will start to shift your mindset from a hesitant "Will I, Won't I?" to a purposeful "I'm on my way"

On Your Journey

Crossing the bridge means personal growth. One of my favourite quotes is from Haruki Murakami: "When you come out of the storm, you won't be the same person who walked in. That's what the storm's all about."

The same is true here–whatever bridge you've decided to cross, you'll be different by the time you get to the other side. Why? Because whatever lies on the other side of the bridge requires something from you: learning, growth, or accepting a new version of yourself.

For me, this is where the mindset piece comes in: adjusting and preparing for what lies ahead and pressing on to your destination. Our brains are hard-wired to keep us safe and comfortable, and crossing the bridge can be anything but that. Sometimes we want to turn back or give up because it's easier—to believe that maybe it wasn't such a good idea after all and that we were better off where we were.

It can take a lot of courage and self-discipline to move forward step by step–neither of them are popular concepts in a world where people would rather things come to them with minimum effort. Progress is often marked not in great leaps and bounds, but in small, consistent steps forward day by day: after a few weeks or a few months, you realized that you've come quite a distance.

Writing my book, I told myself that I needed two weeks away from my day-to-day work to get a good start. Well, guess what: that two week window never seemed to materialize in my diary. It was only when I decided to get up a little earlier and write a couple of hundred words a day that I started to slowly but surely make progress.

There's something else about the bridge: while an actual bridge is usually the shortest distance between two points, life tends to be a bit messier. Things don't go in a straight line. There will always be curveballs, stumbling blocks, and challenges on the way. Crossing the bridge will mean personal change: by the time you get to the other side, you won't be the same person who started. There will be things, as I discovered, to learn, leverage, or leave along the way.

As you cross the bridge, what do you need to learn and do differently when you get to the other side? (for me, it was self-discipline in taking small steps consistently.) What strengths, skills, attributes, and knowledge can you leverage when you get there? (my stubbornness to get things done!) And this is the big one: what do you have to leave behind because it no longer serves you? (my self-doubt and impostor syndrome.)

However driven and determined you are, you're never fully in control. In this life, all of us are making it up as we go along to some degree, and part of the journey is learning to find a balance between making things happen and allowing things to happen, and, in the words of Maya Angelou, learning to "trust life a little bit."

Remember

- Crossing the bridge is about your growth and change on the journey, not just the destination.
- Trust yourself and your inner voice to figure it out... and "trust life a little bit."
- Remember what's on the other side and why you're going there… and keep going.
- Small steps taken consistently are better than leaps and bounds from time to time.

- Finally, DO NOT look at other people on the bridge and think they have it all figured out: they don't. Even if it looks like they do.

Celebrate Your Arrival.

There's a weird thing about arriving on the other side of your bridge: sometimes it might feel like finishing a marathon, with crowds cheering, fireworks rising, and an obvious tape to cross. And sometimes it's a quiet realization of "Oh! I'm here!"

Peas was launched during the pandemic, but I had a day set aside for online launch events, and my kids had strung streamers and balloons around the house to celebrate. My box of books had arrived a few days before, and my son's reaction of "Wow—you wrote a real book!" told me that I'd 'arrived' on the other side.

On the other hand, when I was working full time in a nine-to-five job before I started my own business, I used to imagine a lifestyle where I got to spend time with my kids, attend school sports days, take time off on their school holidays, and so on.

Years later, I was standing on a hill overlooking a beautiful park near my parents' home with the kids playing about nearby, and it occurred to me in a quiet way that I was 'here.' I was taking time out when I wanted to rather than when a boss said I could, and enjoying family time on my own terms.

A feeling of profound gratitude washed over me with that realization.

Friends, life is a series of bridges. Fresh destinations new horizons, and continuous personal growth.

Get to know how the bridge works.

Grow to love the journey.

And take time to celebrate and express gratitude for your wins before moving on.

Adriana Luna Carlos

Founder & CEO of She Rises Studios
Podcast Host | Best Selling Author | #BAUW Movement Creator

https://www.linkedin.com/company/she-rises-studios/
https://www.instagram.com/sherisesstudios/
https://www.facebook.com/sherisesstudios
www.SheRisesStudios.com

Adriana Luna Carlos is a much sought-after expert in Web and Graphic design as well as a new Podcast Host Personnel for She Rises Studios. For over 10 years she has embraced her passion in the digital arts field along with helping women worldwide overcome their insecure idiosyncrasies. Today, when she's not spending time with her family and friends, you'll often find her helping woman focus on rising up and becoming unafraid of success. To learn more about Adriana Luna Carlos and how she can help you overcome obstacles in your business, mindset, or insecurities, visit www.SheRisesStudios.com

HOW TO DREAM BIG AND MAKE YOUR REALITY EVEN BIGGER

By Adriana Luna Carlos

We all know that life can be tough sometimes. But it doesn't mean that you have to just survive; you can become a fighter and use the tough times as an opportunity to grow and learn. As the old saying goes, "If you can dream it, you can do it." But what does that really mean? How do we turn our dreams into reality and never settle for less than we deserve? This is a guide to help you get closer to your goals and make your reality even bigger.

Dreams are an essential part of our lives; they give us something to strive for and keep us motivated. We all have dreams—whether big or small—and sometimes it can be difficult to figure out how to make those dreams come true. It's easy to get caught up in the day-to-day grind and forget about the bigger picture. That's why this guide is here; it will help you break away from that feeling of being stuck and instead focus on achieving your aspirations, no matter how big or small.

The first step in making your dreams a reality is setting achievable goals for yourself. Dreaming big doesn't mean expecting perfection overnight; it means having a plan that will allow you to reach those goals over time. Start by listing all of your long-term objectives and then breaking them down into smaller, more manageable tasks that you can complete one by one until reaching your ultimate goal becomes a reality. Make sure these goals are measurable so that you can track progress and reward yourself when milestones are achieved!

Once you have set goals, create a schedule that works best for you! Everyone moves at their own pace when trying to achieve their ambitions, so be sure to factor in time for rest as well as time dedicated to completing tasks related to fulfilling those goals. When creating this schedule, don't forget about any commitments in your personal life, such as school or work; these should also be taken into consideration when planning out your timetable.

Now comes the hardest part: staying motivated! It may seem like an impossible task, but with some dedication, hard work, and positive thinking, anything is possible! Set reminders on your phone with motivational quotes or images throughout the day so that even if motivation wanes, there is always something there to remind you why continuing on with this journey is important! Also remember not to compare yourself with others; everyone has different paths that lead them towards their final destination, so try not to put too much pressure on yourself because realistically, success doesn't happen overnight—it takes time, energy, and lots of patience!

Finally, never settle for less than what YOU deserve because, at the end of the day, only YOU know what's best for YOU—so, regardless of what others say, push forward because YOU have already dreamed of something greater—make YOUR dreams YOUR reality by taking each step one at a time until you finally reach success! Never forget: If you can dream it, you can do it—so dream big and make your reality even bigger!

Steps on how to make your dreams big and your reality even bigger

- Start by setting big dreams and understanding why it's important to never settle for less than what you truly desire.
- Understand that dreaming big is a great way to increase motivation and achieve your goals.
- Understand why it's important to make your dreams a reality by taking actionable steps.
- Write down the importance of setting realistic goals in order to reach bigger dreams.
- Understand the value of being organized when trying to make

your dreams come true.

- Understand how staying focused on your goals can help you reach them faster.
- Understand the importance of not giving up, even when things get tough—"keep pushing forward"!
- Understand that having a positive attitude can help you achieve your wildest dreams!

It's important to dream big and make sure nothing holds you back from reaching those dreams.

You should always strive for your best potential and never settle for less than what you deserve.

Samantha Lander

SeeFit Living
Functional Diagnostic Nutritionist

https://www.linkedin.com/in/samantha-lander-239a2844/
https://www.facebook.com/seefitpt/
https://www.instagram.com/seefitliving/
www.seefitpt.com

Sam used Functional Diagnostic Nutrition to heal herself from allergies, food sensitivities, hormonal imbalances, and parasites. She's also the founder of SeeFit Living where she coaches people back to optimal health when they just can't quite put their finger on why they feel bad.

She helps educate people about health, diet, stress reduction, rest, and proper supplementation to identify the root cause of why they can't perform at their A-game. S She has been on over 20 podcasts educating people through her own personal journey and education. She is an influencer on social media using that platform to help people learn about health and top products to add into their daily life to optimize their health. She is one of the most authentic and REAL women I have met.

HEALTH IS THE NEW ORANGE

By Samantha Lander

My first advice to anyone reading this is don't judge a book by its cover. I may look like a stereotypical health practitioner, mom, and stand-up human being, but I have not always been that way.

We all define our success, which may or may not include lots of money. People at their lowest of lows can achieve success like no other. For me, the phrase "You can't lose if you don't quit" is always in the back of my head.

I'm a work in progress, like most of us. Currently, I'm a six-figure business owner in recovery from addiction, a felon(yup, I was in prison), not so maternal single mom (hardest job ever), and a health practitioner who wants to help others learn how to be proactive about self-care and optimize their health.

So, hold on to your seat and let me share a little about my life in hopes that it gives you the courage to step out of what is comfortable and go for that crazy "Dream" or "Future Reality" you have always wanted.

As a young girl, I was always a go-getter and followed whatever inspired me at the time. Once, I went to the pool with my mom and saw girls in swimsuits covered in glitter and wearing a beautiful bun, and I knew I wanted to be like that. I did not realize the amount of work it would take to be a successful synchronized swimmer.

But I signed up, and sure enough, a few years later, I won first place in the US for a duet performance.

I visualize myself being the best at whatever I've set out to achieve. Some things, admittedly, have not been the healthiest lifestyle choices, but I always do everything at 110 percent.

Have I failed? UMM, hell yeah.

I had this motto growing up: you must live life to the fullest. However, I had a delusional idea of what that meant, especially during my teenage years.

On paper, I was the model child. I was smart and got good grades. Everyone around me saw what I wanted them to see—a perfect child. In reality, I was partying and wilding as much as I could.

That duality defined my life in a nutshell.

I was the number one rower in the US, went to state for swimming, graduated HS with a 3.8, and attended the University of Michigan (the Harvard of the Midwest). After university, I became one of the top female DJs in LA. Truthfully, I even felt like I was being my best self in prison (yes, I will get to that part soon).

I've come a long way in my journey, and today living life to the fullest means creating my legacy for when I leave this earth. I want to be remembered as the woman who had a dream and went for it even if I might fail. I want to be known for being a good mom; Someone strong, courageous, brutally honest, selfless, and who always put others before themself when it's safe.

I'm on a mission to help others feel like themselves again because I didn't feel that way for years due to underlying health problems. Despite all the physical activities I pushed myself so hard for, I was a very sick child. I had constant stomach problems, and MAN was I always tired. My parents chalked it up to working too hard in sports and left it at that, but I always felt puffy and like I was wearing someone else's skin. This went on for years. I was prescribed various medications but was never given a real diagnosis.

Eventually, I found something that worked to make me feel better.

Drugs. In truth, self-medicating with drugs didn't make me feel better. It just made me *not feel* what was happening in my body. Drugs masked the feeling of ADD and anxiety. I might have been an addict, but at least I didn't feel sick for the first time in my life. I could even eat like a normal person and not get sick.

I was DJ'ing in Los Angeles, producing music, and living a very unhealthy life, but damn it I felt good. Like, *really* good. My dream of being a famous DJ was happening—I just visualized myself being a DJ in front of thousands of people and well, it happened.

If you put it out into the world and see yourself achieving what might seem impossible at the time, it will happen. Is it work? Yes, but you are doing what you love.

My problem was, I also loved drugs. And making money. So, why not sell drugs and be the entrepreneur I knew I was born to be? From the days of selling lemonade as a kid, I always loved being successful, running my own biz, and helping others.

I might have broken a few laws along the way, but I was making people happy and doing what I loved, so that's okay, right? Right and wrong are slippery subjects when your mind is full of fog.

I went from being a small-time drug dealer to realizing monetizing sales meant fewer "buyers" and having one or two "high ticket" clients. Fast forward to the day a full SWAT raid landed me in the LA county jail.

My next chapter began with rehab and 27 months in federal prison. Do I regret my past? NO.

Everything I went through is what brought me to this point. I help others heal, and that has been a driving factor in my entire life. I love what I do. When I got out of prison, I decided to start my own personal training business because who wants to hire a felon?

Did I worry about failing? No.

I visualized my new reality: in one year I would be making six figures because I saw another trainer doing it, so I could too. And I wanted to buy a house. Guess what… I did just that. I built up a clientele and helped men and women get healthier while working on my own health.

Even though I was having great success with male clients, I was still struggling to reach my own health goals. What I learned from my female clientele was that all the hard-hitting go-getters like myself were also battling burnout.

Year after year of doctor visits and hearing, "your labs look fine, nothing is wrong with you" left me feeling unseen and unheard. I was in great shape, but felt terrible all the time. And I was seeing this same pattern in my clients.

The typical calorie in calorie out, do more cardio model was not working. In fact, it was making me feel worse. So I started researching.

That's when I discovered functional lab testing, and it saved my life. Not only did my health turn around, but by applying what I learned, I've been successful at helping thousands of others achieve optimal health.

My guess is you can probably relate to doing all the right things and getting zero results. Maybe you can relate to having hormone imbalances or knowing that your adrenals are shot, and let's not even get started on your gut! I have had at least four parasites that I know of, and I was eating the "perfect diet!" You couldn't pay me to eat something bad, and you know I love to make money.

I learned through functional lab testing that I had over 40 food sensitivities. I was, quite literally, a mess. Sure I was fit, but my body had been on this long roller coaster ride, and it took its toll.

What functional medicine taught me was:

It began with this first lab to introduce me to the unknown world of functional medicine or functional diagnostic nutrition. I dabbled with some holistic doctors in college, so maybe my "gut' was telling me. Here is where I throw in a little educational piece about what and how the heck "Functional Lab testing" goes. I run labs that are not the typical ones you would run at the doctor's.

Basic labs do not discover the root issue, and instead, provide a growing list of medications to cover up symptoms. So then the rollercoaster begins. Some of the symptoms include but are not limited to:

- brain fog
- anxiety
- fatigue
- digestive distress like bloating, diarrhea, SIBO, leaky gut, constipation
- inflammation
- autoimmune conditions
- skin problems
- chronic pain

I am a certified Functional Diagnostic Nutritionist who specializes in uncovering the root cause of WHY you are going through what you are going through in order to offer natural solutions to help you move toward sustainable, long-term healing.

If you're ready to finally feel energized and love life again, then I am your gal. I've been through the sneaky health problems you don't see on a normal lab, and am here to help others in the same boat.

As an entrepreneur, it is hard as hell to run a business! There are days I wish I could just go work in the union and do a 9-5. But that feeling fades fast when I think about the legacy I'm creating.

If I simply gave up would I be following my DREAM?

You know the answer to that.

Today, I am living the life I visualized. I get to change generations of lives by changing the principles in which my clients live, which trickles down into their kids' lives, etc.

It doesn't get much bigger than that.

Nancy Rose

Founder of Quintessence Creations

https://www.facebook.com/nancy.rose.56481
https://embodyyourauthenticself.com/

I've been described as ""determined"" and ""straightforward"" by those that know me. My determination along with my ability to scale challenges provides inspiration to others to fulfill their dreams.

I'm a certified Diamond Light Priestess, energy healer, soul coach, as well as a spiritual minister. I've also lived in the IT corporate world for over 30 years, earned my MBA, worked my way up the ladder, which allows me to understand the challenges women have in this environment. All of these experiences have helped me learn what is NOT me, as well as how I can best serve while not losing myself in the process. My coaching program "Embody Your Authentic Self" is built on what I've learned and helps women return to their true nature and feel alive and fulfilled.

On my personal life, I have 3 children and 3 grandchildren. I live for subtle activism for Mother Earth.

MY JOURNEY TO MY AUTHENTIC SELF

By Nancy Rose

By my mid-thirties, I realized my life was different than most. I was divorced at 33 with three children, and I had an IT career that I loved. And yet, I felt something was missing. I knew there had to be something more to life. And I found it when I read *Celestine Prophecy*. My world opened up. I read and read and read. I found a school where I got my Associate's degree in Metaphysics. I took courses as a healer. I loved this metaphysical world.

And yet I had a dual life. In my corporate job, I was moved into another position every 2-3 years to identify how to mature that function. I realized I had the gift of seeing what needed change. And yet, I wanted to move on once the change was done.

I was struggling to reconcile these two worlds. I felt I had to keep them separate, yet it stifled me. I needed to let both sides of me flourish. I saw the movie *Fifth Element* and again needed to ingrain that in myself. So after a few years, I created my own business, Quintessence Creations. Quintessence is the fifth & highest element in ancient philosophy. It is the essence of a thing in its purest and most concentrated form. That is what I wanted to provide every woman I met.

I loved watching women when they found their connection to their true selves, or what I call their authentic selves. So I continued my search and found tools, since I knew there had to be more. Right around 2012, I found my answers, and that started the birthing of moving towards online courses and coaching since I felt I could reach and help more women that way.

I'm a 'foundation' person. Consider me an explorer and an alchemist. I continue to see what's not working, what is incongruent, and find solutions. And that is how I help each woman that works with me. I help them reconnect with their authentic self, help them release what no longer works, and give them the foundational tools to recenter when times get rough and how to align with their dreams.

So how does that make me unstoppable? I kept searching for what I knew had to exist since the world didn't make sense. I continue to work with the Universe to bring me new connections and ideas, to allow me to give women their foundation to reach the potential of who they truly are. I try to reach as many women as I can.

Because of the different shifts in my life and how I change, people tend to move in and out of my life. The constants in my life are my family. So, I've learned to enjoy the moments I have with those who join me on my journey, for the time being. Parting ways allows each to move in their next direction. I would never want to stop anyone from realizing their dream, whatever road that takes them on. I'm more comfortable now since it's not an end. Instead, they're moments I can cherish.

To me, becoming an unstoppable woman means that I will continue to search to make what I offer women even better. I listen to each one and 'noodle' on any improvements to improve it. Whatever is in my way, whatever doesn't make sense, when I'm trying to figure something out, I figure it out and make things better. I don't give up. I realize sometimes it may take longer than I imagine since everything needs to align. In retrospect, I've gotten so much clarity in why things happened the way they did and the timing. It was perfect. Don't give up on your dream. Understand that there is perfect timing and that you keep taking one step after another, evaluate and change course when needed. The details of your dream may show up differently than you expected or even better than you can imagine.

The most important advice I can give is to trust yourself. If something feels off, listen to your gut—your wisdom—and then ask for the answer to come to you. Pay attention to what comes your way, since it may provide more clarity and direction. Your answer will come, maybe not in your timing, but in Divine Timing. Don't give up on your dream, yet be willing to tune your dream to your new findings.

I want every woman to Meet Their Authentic Self and give them a sampling of what is possible. And everyone reading this book is already connected to the energy to become unstoppable. So I created a special offer that you can get at the link below:

https://embodyyourauthenticself.com/she-rises-unstoppable

Stella Tokar

B.O.L.D. Consulting, LLC
Build-Organize-Lead-Discover
"CEO, IOM, NES, CDP, CPC | Re:Think Clarity Coach

https://www.linkedin.com/in/stella-tokar-b-o-l-d-consulting-llc-3735b013/
https://www.facebook.com/profile.php?id=100009560986214
https://www.facebook.com/BOLDconsultingStella
https://www.instagram.com/stella.tokar/
Rebuilding post pandemic- coming in March 2023
www.BOLDconsulting.com

Public service and ""people"" have always been Stella Tokar's guiding passion for living life professionally and personally. Regardless of stage of life or role, others benefit from her transparent leadership, commitment to excellence, and authenticity. Even while raising her children and following her military officer husband around the world, opportunity presented itself for Stella to make a difference in the lives of others. Mastering transition, she viewed change as an opportunity to reinvent herself and find new ways to lead and be involved.

No matter whether she works alongside the highest of ranking military and civilian leaders, foundations to meet needs of those at the lowest point in life, or anyone in-between, Stella finds fulfillment in living up to her life purpose to advance the welfare of others.

Television host, featured writer, international speaker, coach, professional, wife, mother, and grandmother, Her ability to impact lives shows up wherever she goes.

SADDLE UP!

By Stella Tokar

SADDLE YOUR DREAMS BEFORE YOU RIDE'EM
—Mary Webb

Growing up with horses, I know the value of a saddle for both horse and rider. While protecting the horse's anatomy and providing comfort for riders, it also positions the horse and rider for a better over-all experience together.

The same attributes can be applied when "saddling your dreams" (Mary Webb's words). Properly saddled, the riding experience will have the basic foundation for a better outcome. Saddling your dream is much the same, so choose carefully.

First, you must choose the right saddle. This basic move will set up your riding experience together. Stay real. Don't choose what is popular, on sale, or looks pretty. Keep your needs in mind.

Next, you won't move very far without getting to know your horse. The relationship between the horse and rider is a process. There is a 6th sense that takes over, and no matter what you say… raw emotion is felt, habits form, and that will work for or against you. Know your dream inside and out.

Finally, the learned strategy to ride transforms into the power to lead in any situation. You and your horse become one through a bond of trust. When saddling your dreams, building blocks of trust for achieving allows you to command any situation that comes up along the way confidently. Self-assured, you learn to pivot, and your hands never come off the reins. You influence the outcome.

Now, let's use the same steps to saddle up your dream and take this ride together. You can't put your "DO" to work without the "DREAM" firmly in place.

REALITY – THE PLATFORM TO BUILD IT

Define your reality and put it in writing.

The first responsibility you have to yourself and your dream is to define your current reality. Don't be afraid to ask powerful questions that expose your truth. Only then can you address the findings honestly and intentionally use them to move toward your dream.

Don't think about where you should or desire to be. Instead, get descriptive on what "right now" looks like. Without this transparency process, you can only make assumptions that will lead you blindly to who-knows-where.

The platform you build must be solid to move from delusion to conclusion. A flawed foundation will begin to fracture in the smallest of ways that you won't even notice. You will go through the many sequences of your dream, and as time passes and the pressures of life come and go, the weight of external elements will challenge your vision. If the foundation is not developed properly, it will fail to support and sustain the reality of achieving it. If that breakdown occurs, you will begin to compromise its integrity and, once fractured, it will not hold. A strong reality check is your opportunity for a strong platform base.

Reality Check 101: Build It

- What is my dream and where will it take me?
- What steps am I willing to take to build on my current reality?
- How can I change or improve?
- Does my foundation connect and support my dream?
- Who / what will it impact?
- How will I measure progress?

HABITS - THE PROCESS TO MOVE IT

"We are what we repeatedly do.
Excellence, then, is not the act, but a habit."
—Aristotle

It is no secret that repeated behavior forms a habit.

But did you know there is a science behind intentionally forming good habits? By exposing our harmful habits, we can renew our brains/minds to default to new and healthy habits we create to take their place.

We each have amazing power and ability within us called neuroplasticity. When we are aware of the brain's ability to structurally rearrange itself in response to varied experiences, we can take our thoughts captive and renew them. These experiences allow our brain's nerve cells to change physically. So, if we want positive habits, we work toward creating a mindset that creates positive experiences. This is very intentional. Coaching my clients through the reality check sets them up for this reset of their minds. They are amazed at how quickly it takes place. As a Neuroencoding specialist, I could tell you more about this exciting process, but, for now, I just want you to know that YOU have the ability and power over this process. I will share more in my upcoming book.

Habits form out of our natural self and are swayed through learned behaviors and external influence. All this has everything to do with how you dream. Dreaming takes courage. Your ability to believe in yourself will impact your ability to capture your dreams. And for some, the process of simply dreaming is compromised because of their habits. Whatever masters your mind drives your behavior.

Habit Check 101: Move It

- To think well, I must live well.
    - What changes do I need for healthy thinking and creating healthy habits to dream bigger?

- I will create time every day to focus on my dream.
  - What time of day?
  - Where will I be?
  - How will I move my dream forward daily?
  - Who is included in making that dream reality?
- What habits are weights? Hold me back.
- What habits are wings? Propel me forward.
- What steps will I take today to create new healthy habits?
- What is the cost I am willing to pay for my dream?

MINDSET -THE POWER TO ACHIEVE IT

"…dream big dreams, …and believe in possibilities, …put yourself in a position to achieve them."
—John Maxwell

Mindset…this is the hard drive within you. So, the question becomes: "Is the power of your mindset bringing you closer to your dream?"

All your life decisions process through the brain, which is an organ of your body. But the mind resides in the soul, the heart of who you are and where your beliefs and values form and dwell.

That power sets in motion all the programs you have booted up in your mind's hard drive. Thinking drives actions and actions become behaviors.

The mind will default less to thinking about what is impossible when it has a healthy program to run on. In John's quote, two things are mentioned for a powerful mindset to be achieved: 1) belief and 2) positioning yourself. Notice one is internal, and one is external.

1) BELIEF

What you believe influences how you live. There is a difference between a strong, healthy mindset and plain stubborn will. Willfulness is driven by emotion, and we all know how unstable that can be. A mindset is molded through intentional processes based on self-awareness and beliefs.

Believe sincerely in what is possible, and the view of your dream will be unobstructed.

Trust yourself and build confidence. Trusting is risk-taking. What lies ahead is unclear but your mindset needs to see it as an opportunity and meet the future with great expectations. Don't be afraid to fail. Failure provides golden learning nuggets that offer prospectivenew ways of thinking about achievement and ways to supersize our dreams.

Mindset Check 101: Achieve It - Belief

- What is my greatest area of need when it comes to self-trust, and how do I leverage it?
- How do you measure risk?
- How and why am I trustworthy?
- What are my beliefs and values, and do they connect to my dream(s)?

2) POSITION YOURSELF

Intention yields purpose.

When was the last time you asked yourself, "What do I want?" That answer needs to be clear. You can't take a journey if you are unsure of the destination. To position yourself, you must have clarity on your purpose.

We are all born to start life from different vantage points. That's okay. We all have equal ability to create a powerful mindset on purpose and seize opportunities. The difference between those who do and those who don't is how they see themselves and what they do with their circumstances.

Learn to pivot when you are outside your comfort zone, challenged, or make a mistake. The smallest of adjustments can make a huge difference. Calculated carefully, your position becomes stronger, and you develop a better version of yourself. The right attitude about every situation leads you to opportunity. Opportunity seized reveals a new approach to the achievement of your dream. The question becomes, "What do I want?"

Mindset Check 101: Achieve It - Power, Purpose, Position

- What do I want?
- My mindset will get me to my dream.
    - If not, why?
- Challenges, mistakes, failure…how do I pivot?
- What am I waiting on/for?

Remember to sit tall in your saddle.

1. Reality Check - definition will support building a strong platform to build the dream.
2. Habits are the process of moving your dream and sustaining it.
3. A mindset of healthy beliefs drives purpose and creates a powerful position to achieve your dream.

Got Dreams? Ride'em cowgirl!

Gail Meriel

Success Redefined
Mindset Coach

https://www.linkedin.com/in/gail-meriel-mba-pmp-6943894/
https://www.facebook.com/profile.php?id=100086619168792
www.gailmeriel.com

Gail Meriel is a Project Manager, International Best-Selling Author, award-winning Motivational Speaker, and Mindset Coach. She is a Sr. Consultant with Unify Consulting, LLC, and is the Founder of Success Redefined. She has an MBA degree and Project Management Certification, and over 25 years of corporate experience with Fortune 500 companies. Gail helps inspire and empower women who lost confidence or feel unworthy from failure and self-doubt learn how to regain their confidence through self-discovery and overcome imposter syndrome so they can take controllable action, redefine their success and become Warriors with a Purpose. Connect with Gail on LinkedIn, Facebook, Clubhouse and www.gailmeriel.com to learn how she can help you in your journey to redefine YOUR Success. Gail lives in the Chicago area with her husband Joe and golden retriever Cubby. Her greatest accomplishment is her son Ryne, to whom she is building her legacy.

BECOME A WARRIOR WITH A PURPOSE

By Gail Meriel

I saw myself doing the catwalk on a fashion show runway, trying not to trip while walking on high heels (think Sandra Bullock's Miss Congeniality-style trip), soaking in the flashing cameras and applause as I showcase the latest fashion trends. I also saw myself being a news anchor for a Chicago television network. While I read a ton of books in my childhood, I also dreamed of one day being a writer. Some may call these typical big childhood dreams, but as I grew older, I held back from actively pursuing them. A few decades ago, my chances of being a fashion model or broadcaster were unlikely. The industry landscape was not as diverse as it is now. I experienced what is now known as imposter syndrome, which prevented me from going for those dreams despite the odds. What are my chances of being accepted into these fields? I didn't feel I was enough. The models in magazines or television did not look like me—a petite Filipina American. I didn't fit the traditional standard profile of women in those industries. According to a January 20, 2022 article from shiftlondon.org, most of the biggest and most successful models from the 1990s, 2000s, and even 2010s have been slim and white.[1] Although Connie Chung was the first Asian American to anchor a major network newscast in the U.S., the industry had a long way to go for Asian women's visibility to be the norm. External narratives I heard didn't help my self-confidence. I've personally been told to 'go back to my country' and experienced micro-aggressions even though I was born in Chicago. I felt I didn't belong with others, so why even try?

------

[1] Alavi, Ayza. "The Evolution of the Modeling Industry." *Shiftlondon.org,* 20 Jan. 2022

When it was time to choose my career path, I took the route that made sense based on industry demand and my natural skillset. I went into technology, and my journey took me to project management. Of course, my career wasn't perfect—it had its ups and downs. The projects I managed were very fulfilling and impactful. I gained prestige and respect in the industry for my work. I won corporate awards for my leadership, and I was extremely proud when I saw my project featured as a Super Bowl commercial. Throughout my career, the challenges were hard to bounce back from mentally, especially when there was a workforce reduction or restructuring. Imposter Syndrome crept back up. Being restructured into a new role or new management, I felt I had to prove myself more as a professional to get to where I wanted to be. Management styles sometimes didn't align, and I struggled to keep up. When I failed multiple times, success became more and more difficult, to the point of burnout. One of the greatest gifts I was given was being a mom—I wouldn't trade it for the world. But there were times when I had to choose priorities between my career and family. If I chose the wrong proverbial door to enter, I would be committing career suicide (as I was advised by leadership would happen), or my own internal voice and guilt for not having time for my son would invade my thoughts. The remote work format was not accepted as a corporate standard yet. Even well into the millennium when work from home became the norm, the boundaries between work and personal life became blurry. I was doing well in my career, advancing with promotions, and getting visibility to executive leadership. But I didn't enjoy the opportunity cost of chasing titles and not having a fulfilling personal life. My mental, emotional, and physical health started to suffer—how can I be everything to everyone AND take care of myself? I knew I needed a Plan B.

I decided to start my deep soul-searching journey. The advantage of going through so many challenges is being able to implement strategies that helped me stay optimistic while figuring out how to make my dreams a reality and not lose myself in the process.

1) **Prioritize ME:** I learned to give myself some grace—I absolutely deserved it! Cultural and gender norms I grew up with dictated being a servant leader to anyone who needed it—family, friends, colleagues, corporate management, etc. Saying no when my plate was already full was a sign of weakness, and the societal definition of success was being able to handle that and more. Being a perfectionist and high achiever are not titles I wanted to continue holding. Sadly, it took a series of illnesses (thanks to genetics, stress, and anxiety) I experienced for me to realize I needed to change. I want to be here in the now, especially for my family. I learned to prioritize myself so I can BE myself to others. I carved out time for myself. Once I started implementing that strategy, I didn't want to go back! I committed to going to the spa at least once a quarter, allowed myself a day or two (or three) of a weekend putzing around the house in PJs all day to binge-watch, and committed myself to try new work-out routines so I'm motivated to continue working toward my fitness goals, especially when I plateau. Life will always have its hills and valleys, and I learned to recharge my batteries so I can bring my whole, stronger, warrior self when I need to go into combat mode to face challenges. In addition, the mighty force and energy of positive human interaction is another key I unlocked to dreaming big and doing bigger. Connecting with others who build me up gives me a different perspective on challenges. Having mentors to help guide me and spending quality time with family and friends boosts my self-esteem, and desire to improve my situation.

2) **Redefine Success:** My soul-searching journey led me to a process that I would later find was a pattern. It always led me

to the same questions—what really is my 'Why?' Is it different than it was when I first sought this goal? When I started a family? What did I want to achieve from my goals? The answers to those questions led me to dig deeper and assess what I could and could not control. I couldn't control how the world around me was changing and how people view me, but I could control how I reacted to those factors. I searched for the career leadership style that resonated with me and matched my leadership style. I dug up my childhood dreams to figure out what I really wanted and why I wanted to pursue them in the first place. Are they possible now, or are they still the wild dreams that can only live in my heart and soul? I redefined my success by shifting my mindset and perspective. I want to continue the leadership path while prioritizing myself and my family. Was there a more creative way to show my leadership and be an influencer? Journaling my goals, celebrating my successes, documenting challenges and roadblocks, and memorializing my 'Why' created a framework to clear my mind, set my emotions aside, and determine a realistic path forward.

3) **Go For It and Push Boundaries to Fulfill Dreams:** The mental exercise I went through to help redefine my success led me to go for it. I now have a different perspective on boundaries I perceived were blockers in pursuing. I committed myself to being a leader without sacrificing myself. I love my career as a project manager, but that doesn't mean my dreams stop there. If COVID taught me anything, it is that life is short, and now is the time to go for my dreams. Through my self-discovery, I found a purpose through those dreams and am finding creative ways to achieve them. What's my 'Why?' I want to change lives, represent, inspire and empower others, and build my family legacy.

As children, we are taught by our parents, teachers, and media that we can be anyone we want. Of course, life happens, and sometimes we must put those dreams aside. We will never be ready. There will be no perfect time to pursue what we always wanted to do. There will always be people who discourage us through their negative language. But we are warriors, and our shield will protect us. We can remove our self-doubt, push the boundaries of what we are capable of, and commit to it. We can showcase our strengths to be the best versions of ourselves and change the world. It all starts with the mindset shift. I invite you to join me in this life-long journey of dreaming big to find purpose and meaning in our lives, which will push us to do bigger and beat the odds. We will become Warriors with a Purpose.

Andrea Kaye

Certified Magnetic Mind Coach | Making the Shift
Magick Miracles & Alchemy | Quantum Manifestation & Spiritual
Mindset Coaching | Making Dreams Reality

https://www.facebook.com/andrea.shive
https://making-the-shift.com/
https://andreashive.com/

Hi, I'm Andrea. I am a superconscious creator & Transformation accelerator. I help you awaken to your divine soul truth, find your purpose & take your power back.

I help mompreneurs & spiritual entrepreneurs specifically, to overcome limited programming & manifest their dreams.

I am a 36 year old home birthing unschooling mompreneur of 4 Transformational Master Quantum Manifestation Coach Spiritual Mindset Mentor Intuitive Healer & Akashic Records Practitioner certified in Neurolinguistic Programming Emotional Freedom Tapping & Time Techniques Life & Success Coaching as well as Hypnotherapy & the Magnetic Mind Method

I'm also the Fearless Humble leader of Miracle Mavens helping moms create time & financial freedom.

My personal mission is to transform the world one person at a time starting with myself.

We are being dumbed down drugged up & disempowered & I am committed to helping people awaken to their full potential & raising the vibration of the planet to shift us into the new 5D paradigm ""heaven on earth"".

HOLY SHIFT! I AM THE BRIDGE

By Andrea Kaye

Ready to unlock magical manifesting powers and make your dreams reality? Well, you're in the perfect place, and it's no accident you picked up this book. It just so happens this is exactly what I specialize in. Making Dreams Reality is the name of my Facebook group.

In November 2017, I started shopping at an online wellness store. I began my spiritual awakening, self-discovery, personal development, and healing journey. I often compare myself to Chinese bamboo, which grows underground for five years. When it finally breaks through the surface, it shoots up over 90 feet in the first few weeks.

In the five years of my journey, I faced many challenges. There were many setbacks, disappointments, and failures, but I pressed forward because I had a massive vision. I developed unshakeable faith in my calling and purpose. I faced my fears head-on.

I was a single mother much of that time and have since healed my relationship with the father of our now four children. I also had my first two unassisted homebirths in this period. They were very powerful experiences, especially after having a C-section and VBAC with the first two and five miscarriages prior to that. That's another story for another day.

In 2019 I had a dream. I saw the seven chakras. They are the seven energy centers in your body and are the colors of the rainbow. I saw them in a vertical line in the sky, and Pegasus jumped through. A few weeks later, I dreamt of hundreds of doves flying above me back and forth. Both of these dreams were interpreted to mean success, inner peace, and freedom.

A few months after having these dreams, I went to have a unicorn reading in a little crystal shop. This beautiful, highly intuitive woman told me, without knowledge of my dream, that I have a Pegasus guide and Pegasus is the bringer of truth. She told me my life was about to change, that I would be successful beyond anything I've ever imagined, and it would happen SO FAST it would seem overwhelming. I have since been watching magic and miracles unfold in my life.

In January 2020, I decided to become a coach to have the tools to help more people transform their lives. I became obsessed with personal and spiritual development. I followed my passion. I didn't make excuses. I took action to create my dreams. I love the saying those who are afraid of doing too much often do too little. Fear will stop you in your tracks, but fear is an illusion—false evidence appearing real.

Dream Big Do Bigger is about taking consistent action in your daily life that compounds into massive momentum and results over time. Like the Chinese bamboo or anything you plant, the day you plant the seed isn't the day you eat the fruit. Rome wasn't built in a day. Creation takes time.

We live in a 3D reality where it takes time to move through space. If our thoughts and words manifested instantly, the world would be even stranger than the one we currently know. I mean, what is all this anyway? What is our purpose?

Well, I believe we are spiritual beings having a human experience. We come here to experience life, learn, grow, expand, and evolve. Earth is a ground for spiritual growth and soul evolution. We come here to awaken to our true divine spiritual nature and master our intuitive gifts.

Your purpose is something personal to you, unique, and will reveal itself over many lifetimes. (Lifetimes because you are a spirit— energy—and energy doesn't die. It transforms.) Your purpose provides for you. It's spiritual, and the purpose of it all is the EXPANSION of the infinite, eternal universe we are all a part of.

I believe we are one consciousness, one body, or one mind. We are all aspects of this one awareness experiencing life in a multitude of fashions. You are an extension of that which we have come to know as "God," the source of all creation. It is an infinite, eternal, quantum field of pure, creative, conscious energy. We are all connected to it and to each other. What we call it is only a label. Labels limit all that this truly is.

We are powerful creators creating on behalf of this source which is pure unconditional love and light. We have forgotten who we are, and our minds have created fear. Fear is the opposite of love. Light and dark are both within you, and you get to choose which you serve: Love or fear, worry or faith, but you cannot serve two masters. Fear and love cannot coexist.

Everything in this universe is energy, frequency, and vibration and these are all levels on the emotional scale. Fear is the lowest, and anger, unforgiveness, resentment, bitterness et cetera all lead to anxiety or depression and disease in the body.

High vibrations are healing to the body. When you vibrate on the frequency of love, you are one with "God." Love is the highest vibration in the universe, along with gratitude, peace, joy, et cetera. These are the frequencies of 5D consciousness.

Most people store their energy in the root chakra, the lowest energy center in the body, in the third dimension of the material world. This keeps you in fear and survival and depletes the electromagnetic field around your heart. You are more matter and less energy like this. You will find yourself trying to force everything in your life because you are out of alignment energetically.

That was a lot of information! Truth is, everything is information. Light, frequency, and vibration all carry information within an invisible field that surrounds us. The quantum field or the unseen spiritual realms are like WiFi; you can't hear, see, smell, touch, or taste it, but it's there. When we tap into this, we have access to infinite and limitless possibilities for our lives.

Our thoughts are energy, our emotions are energy in motion, and according to universal law, the laws of God, your mind is a magnet. You attract experiences according to what you believe and how you feel. Your mindset creates your reality. You are emitting a vibrational signal into the field and it is mirrored back to you in physical reality.

You are creating your reality whether you are aware of it or not. Most people are creating subconsciously based on old, outdated programming and limiting beliefs. These programs are learned at an early age, from past experiences, trauma, or things passed down generationally.

This is only a portion of everything I've learned since deciding to become a coach. I took many courses, and I am certified in several processes to help others shift their mindset to make their dreams reality.

As a Multidimensional Quantum Manifestation Coach & Spiritual Mindset Mentor certified in the Magnetic Mind Method, I use the five steps to conscious creation superconscious transformation recodes. This work is based on ancient Hermetic principles, alchemy, universal law, epigenetics, quantum physics, and proven neuroscience. It rewires the brain to release resistance so you can be in flow and become the magnet for your dreams.

Truth is, you are the only thing in your way. You can have, be, and do anything; you've just got to decide and take action. Intentional, aligned action using brain and heart coherence works best. Clear intention with an elevated emotion such as gratitude will help you quantum leap in the creation process.

You see, you are the creator of your own reality, and you get to choose what you create. There is a process to creation that most are unaware of, plus all the unconscious limiting beliefs, old identities, and the false programming blocking you. This keeps you stuck in karmic loops creating the very things you say you don't want.

Dream Big Do Bigger is about taking radical responsibility for your free will and choice. It's about self-awareness. The "I am" awareness. Realizing that you are the bridge. Holy SHIFT! I AM the bridge. Your thoughts, feelings, and emotions create your decisions, and your decisions create your life.

All the suffering you have endured is meant to awaken you to your power. When you rise to the challenges and learn to transmute your pain to purpose rather than blame or play victim, you become the alchemist, the creator of your own life experience. It's about doing the inner work instead of avoiding the uncomfortable pain attached to growth. Then you take action from a place of alignment. You create from the inside out.

This is how miraculous transformation occurs and how you make your dreams a reality. This is my truth and my message to the world. You are a powerful creator, and you get to choose what you create. You are worthy, and you are more than enough. Love is the answer. Truth, Love, and Light. Namaste.

Dr. Ola Abbas

Elevate Your Health & Wealth
Consultant

https://www.linkedin.com/in/drolaabbas/
https://www.facebook.com/groups/thewealthytravelcommunity/
https://www.instagram.com/elevatewithola/
https://elevatewithola.com/maximzeyourpotential

"Your only limit is the limit you place on yourself"
—Dr. Ola Abbas

Dr. Ola Abbas is a dual accredited Consultant in Critical care and Acute medicine working in the National Health Service in the UK.

She was born and raised in Iraq, forced to leave her home country after the turmoil of the war to eventually settle in England. Ola found herself having to re-establish her roots, and rebuild herself from the ground up.

Ola has ventured into entrepreneurship to enable her to help more people rise to their potential. She runs a successful travel business, coaching and mentoring over 100 professionals on how to create their wealth and well-being from travel.

She is on a mission to build a progressive, diverse and inclusive community that thrives on empowering peers to attract the Clarity, Confidence, Community & Cash they desire and deserve into their lives.

YOU WERE BORN LIMITLESS

By Dr. Ola Abbas

In 2003, I lived in Iraq, where I was born and raised. At that time, I believed where I was in life was my limit. I believed I would be living there for the rest of my life, that I'd finish studying medicine and become a family doctor with a clinic down the road from where I lived. I was happy with that.

The war and its consequences made it near-to-impossible for my family and me to stay there. We were forced to leave and find safe refuge. That meant I had to leave behind many of the people and things that were a part of my life and my limiting beliefs of who I am and can be.

I had to restart, rebuild, and redefine myself. I lived between Dubai and Lebanon for some years before settling in the UK. The road wasn't paved with roses—it was one hoop of fire after another with a fair number of setbacks.

Where many would have called it a day and settled for less than what they deserved and lived within a certain limit, I chose to channel my unlimited inner potential to create a life and an existence that matches my worth and my values.

I moved mountains and carved my career path in a male-dominated industry. I qualified as a dual accredited Consultant in critical care and acute medicine, and I took a substantive post at a highly sought-after tertiary neurosciences and trauma hospital in the Northwest of England.

Many would have accepted that as the ultimate career pinnacle and stopped there. That would have been totally acceptable as the limit of one's career and/or potential. I, however, felt that there was more. The Universe is abundant and limitless. We are creatures of this Universe, and as such, we are abundant and limitless.

Build Your Own Table!

While I have reached great heights personally and professionally, it wasn't without paying the tax. I was bullied for being different, looking different, and wanting different things in my life.

My race, religion, looks, and being a female meant I had to work extra hard to prove that I was worthy of a seat at the table. I sometimes didn't get a seat at the table regardless of how hard I worked.

The choice was to succumb to the limit imposed on me or to challenge it and break the glass ceiling. I did the latter. I chopped the wood and built my own table.

I realized that I was different, not in how my looks make me stand out but in how I can see and create a vision for life, a vision others can't see. I knew I had this great potential in me, and to limit it would be the ultimate selfish act.

The seating at my table carries the label "come as you are." You don't need to look a certain way. You are embraced and celebrated for being different, for doing differently, and most importantly, for dreaming big and making the dream happen.

The Universe Gives You What You Need When You Need It

Our differences as humans have always intrigued me. The cultures we live in shape us to be who we are, the languages we speak, and the way we express (or bottle up) emotions.

Being someone who has always been judged and bullied for being different, I sought to normalize differences by traveling and exploring different cultures.

Travel awards many gains; the most impactful is making us more tolerant of others regardless of how different they are. It allows us to develop a different attitude and a broader mindset for accepting people and what they bring to the table rather than judging their looks even before they pull up a chair.

The opportunity to travel more, to make travel a lifestyle, and to develop myself into a travel business consultant and mentor came my way like an answer to a prayer I longed for.

I grabbed the bull by the horns and ran with it. It's one thing to dream about creating a change in your life, however it's a completely different thing to put your dreams into action and witness the change unfold.

I knew that I just had to take that first step, have faith in myself, and that the Universe gave me what I needed when I needed it.

Going Back to the Drawing Board

The thing about restarting your journey, flipping a page, and writing a new chapter is that you never restart from scratch. You don't go back to ground zero, though the disappointment of having to restart might make it feel like that.

You are going back to the drawing board with the experience you accumulated, the resilience you developed, and the knowledge of what to do and not do on a bigger and better scale.

Working as a high-flying Consultant in healthcare is an admirable role. I love healing my patients and helping them recover from life-limiting injuries and illnesses that could have killed them in a heartbeat. Yet, such a role comes with a sizeable burden of moral injury*, more so during the Covid pandemic and its aftermath.

To say that all the skeletons that I shoved away in the back of my closet come out is an understatement.

I suffered a significant wave of post-traumatic stress. I was forced to pause and re-examine my big dream. After healing, I started to rechart my course again. Yes, I can still continue in my job, yet I am feeling pulled and called to a bigger mission—to do bigger and to help others dream big and do bigger. I want to help them reach their potential, to be more, have more, and give more.

Trauma from a job (or relationship) doesn't have to be the end of it, nor the end of you.

Moral injury: when someone engages in, fails to prevent, or witnesses acts that conflict with their values or beliefs. Examples of events that may lead to moral injury include:

- *Having to make decisions that affect the survival of others or where all options will lead to a negative outcome.*
- *Doing something that goes against your beliefs (referred to as an act of commission)*
- *Failing to do something in line with your beliefs (referred to as an act of omission)*
- *Witnessing or learning about such an act*
- *Experiencing betrayal by trusted others*

Source: National Center for PTSD

Your Only Limits Are the Ones You Place on Yourself.

You can have an unlimited bank of excuses that limit you, or you can have unlimited success.

You can let your race, religion, looks, weight, language, accent, capability, or disability limit you, or wear them as your superpower.

Learn to flip your excuse story into a success story:

- Dream big and have a plan to act on your dream.
- The perfect time is now, in Nike's words, "Just do it."
- Small steps create change faster than big leaps.
- Comparisonitis is a dangerous disease; trust the timing of when things will happen.

- Hone your strengths instead of wasting time on your weaknesses.
- Expect to fail, but remember that failure is life rerouting you back to the path of success.

Yes, You Can.

I'm here not only to tell you you can do it, but also to show you how.

If I immigrated from under gunshots, bombs, and terror attacks and ended up where I am now, then you can have and achieve anything. I remember hiding under the stairwell while bombs were flung over the city, thinking to myself: "Am I going to live for another day?"

I not only lived and healed from the trauma, I thrived. Along the way, I discovered the formula for thriving with limitless potential, and I am now making it my mission to share it with others.

You won't know it all on day one, and you won't know all the answers as you walk your limitless journey. You must trust the process, and have faith in yourself and in that the Universe has your back.

Whenever you think you have reached your limit, take stock of what you have with a grateful heart and reach out to a new limit. You are a divine being of this abundant Universe with unlimited potential, and you, my darling, were born limitless.

P.S. I'm including free access to the *Maximize Your Potential Quiz*. After taking the quiz, you'll be able to download your *Bespoke Limitless Roadmap*, click here for the quiz.

https://elevatewithola.com/maximzeyourpotential

Michelle Bell

CEO of Virtual Work Wife™

https://www.linkedin.com/company/virtual-work-wife
https://www.facebook.com/virtualworkwife
https://www.instagram.com/virtualworkwife/
www.virtualworkwife.com
www.michellebell.com

Michelle Bell is the CEO of Virtual Work Wife, a Marketing Agency that is anything but typical.

With a specialty in workflow and process automation, our agency is providing personalized solutions for any size business seeking to create more balance.

Founded to help busy entrepreneurs like herself find creative solutions so they could work around their family schedule rather than scheduling family around work, our core values are:

Work less - Make more - Do the things you love.

By focusing on strategic solutions, wholistically balanced campaigns, and the belief that authentic marketing will always win over formulas, the Agency provides a one-stop-shop for client care and jobs where talent is fostered and growth is encouraged.

Lifting people up into their own success stories is what gets me out of bed in the morning. Being of service and surrounding yourself with clients, and friends, who share in your core values is the true measure of accomplishment.

VIRTUAL WORK WIFE, THAT'S A COOL NAME. WHAT DOES IT MEAN?

By Michelle Bell

A long a$$ time ago, I started Virtual Work Wife because a) I wanted to be the one raising my kids and 2) I wanted to do things my own way. But mostly a.

I was totes jealous of how much time the sitter had with my kid. It should have been *my time*. Sammie would be asleep when I dropped her off and cranky when I picked her up. Being a part-time mommy sucked butt!

So, I started an at-home business supporting entrepreneurs—the ones who couldn't afford to hire full-time support. Since then, we've grown into a full-scale marketing agency.

Now, nearly 20 years later, I still get asked where the name Virtual Work Wife came from.

Honestly, I didn't realize it at the time, but the name says everything about how our agency runs.

I was working for a large corporation, often putting in 16-hour days and doing all the typical overachiever things one does to get ahead. This was way before the days of #actyourwage.

I had a work husband. You know, the one person you *actually like* seeing at work. The one who has your back and helps you get sh*t done. My lunch buddy who had all the good gossip about the slackers.

Let me just say, working for the man sucks! Yet, all my life, my grandpa said, "get a good job at a stable company that offers a pension." Work your 20 and retire comfortably. #boomers, am I right?

Meanwhile, I did what he said; it was the suckiest six years of my life! My grandpa didn't tell me how miserable every day would be, or that all the "perks" came with a price.

Dressing like a lady, having to conform, playing by the rules, being nice, blah blah blah.

Corporate politics was exhausting and miserable.

I lost my job six years into my 20-year prison sentence, and it was a blessing. I knew I didn't want to keep doing what I was doing but I hadn't figured out how to break free. I was determined to find another job but wanted something closer to home that offered flexibility and didn't expect 16-hour days.

Yeah, no. Stop laughing. I learned unicorn jobs don't exist.

After a wonderful day of playing with my daughter and truly enjoying being at home, I finally owned up to never wanting to work for *the man* again.

So naturally, I called my bestie and told her everything so she could like, you know, fix it for me. Because that's in the bestie rulebook. She said I should just start my own business.

Cue the fear and years of indoctrination.

"I can't."

Why? She asked. Let's see ... "because I need insurance, I have a baby, and I need a 401k."

Do you know what she said to me?

"Why can't you get that stuff yourself?"

I sat there in stunned silence for a while. You might have guessed by now, I'm not really the silent type, y'all. But there I was, legitimately frozen while my mind fought to unlearn years of conformity and dependence on a system meant to hold people back.

That moment of clarity changed my life! I was free. I could control my destiny.

I didn't need anyone to do it for me. I didn't have to sell my soul for healthcare and a pension plan. I just had to be brave.

And thus, Virtual Work Wife was born.

With one client (a referral from my bestie), a shitty laptop, and a TV tray for a desk, I did the thing. I started a home-based business. #socialdistancingsince2005

Initially, choosing the name Virtual Work Wife seemed cute and funny, like me :)

It was a nod to the fact that the _only thing_ I would miss about corporate life was my work husband.

I knew plenty of small businesses couldn't afford to hire a full-time assistant. They probably missed having a work wife/husband too, and they really needed more than a secretary. They needed a virtual ride or die.

Something happened that I didn't realize at the time, but it truly shaped my mission statement and set the tone for how I would grow my business into what it is today.

In that moment, I chose how I was going to work with clients. When you think about it, there are only two kinds of client relationships:

- Clients are transactions
- Clients are partnerships

Without consciously realizing it, I chose to make clients partners. The way I see it when prospective clients come to us for help, they aren't hiring someone just to do stuff or magically fix all their problems. They are looking for strength in numbers. They are looking for support and validation that their business can be everything they want it to be.

We, as consultants, have the power to set the tone for the relationship. We can either accept being treated as contractors—a transaction with an expiration date—or, own our expertise and act as equals in an ongoing consultancy.

I am simply not interested in being treated like a transaction or treating others that way. That's how _the man_ does business. I am different. Better.

As partners, we are invested in seeing our clients achieve and exceed their goals.

However, I refuse to chase someone into being successful. We expect our clients to be committed to the process. They need to invest more than a consulting fee. They must be present and contribute to the project's overall success.

My daughter likes to call it matching energies. Remember the reason I started all this, well she's 22 now and earned a Masters's degree in Criminal Justice. After years of being my assistant, she wants to do her own thing. #sothedrama

Where was I, oh yeah; clients must put in as much time and energy as we are for success to happen. It's non-negotiable. We are going to create and execute a plan on your behalf, but you will be a part of it. There's going to be homework, and you're gonna do that homework because that's the only way all of us will meet our goals.

We can give a client all the tools and a roadmap to their dream business, but it still has to be their voice, their message. To create true authenticity, you can't take shortcuts.

We don't sell magic pills. If you want that, check your Facebook feed. But beware, it's far too easy to waste your entire budget buying shortcuts. If you spend $200-$300 dollars and it doesn't work, it's okay. It was an acceptable risk.

But those things add up. They drain your funds and your spirit.

Successful entrepreneurs understand they can't be absent from their businesses. They have to be in the process.

If they don't share that belief, then they can't work with us. And that's okay, too.

I learned along the way it's okay to say no.

No, you are not a good fit for us. No, we are not a good fit for you.

Ultimately, saying no is doing everyone a favor. When you say yes to the jobs you don't feel good about, it only leads to resentment and making work feel like *work… and no one wants that!*

Success breeds success. We create brighter futures for our clients and in turn, they create opportunities for us. That can take many forms. Sometimes it's a referral. Sometimes, when the chemistry is right, it leads to collaborations.

Collaborations are the best possible outcome.

When we've built an automated workflow and marketing system, we look at the finished product and ask ourselves, is this repeatable? Is this something other businesses within the niche can benefit from, and can our client benefit from reselling it?

If the answer is yes, and the relationship is enjoyable, we have the opportunity to create a new entity. A micro-business. Equal partners where we are the tech and the client is the expert. Together we can sell a product that moves an industry or niche forward. It's a recipe for success that has infinite possibilities.

It's more than just info marketing. Anyone can sell their "exact method" for making 200 calls in a day. This is the next level. We're taking the marketing tech and packaging it with industry expert coaching to help grow businesses.

What are you doing in your business that could be packaged and resold? Is it scalable? Do you have the tech expertise to build it and the voice to teach it? Or do you need a strategic partner to help you move forward?

To dream big is easy; to do bigger takes planning, expertise, and the ability to know when you need help. Take advantage of the potential partnerships in your ecosystem, and you'll be doing bigger in no time!

So what is a Virtual Work Wife?

It's a person, a brand, and a lifestyle! Virtual Work Wife is a full-service marketing agency that helps small businesses achieve their goals while making work fun.

We help industry leaders like you communicate ideas in a way that makes your ideal customer stand up, pay up, and pay attention.

I founded Virtual Work Wife because I believe two things are true:

- you can have a successful business and still put your family first.
- telling your authentic truth is the best way to lead, inspire, and persuade your ideal customer into joining you.

And I believe that most email marketing is too long and too boring! We can do better.

Colleen McCartney

Holistic Tech & Wellness Coach

https://www.linkedin.com/company/totally-essential
https://www.facebook.com/TotallyEssential
https://www.instagram.com/totally.essential
https://colleenmccartney.com/
https://thewellnesscrm.com/

Born and raised in Northern Virginia with a heart for adventure, Colleen is a wife, dog mom, and aunt to nine tiny humans. Throughout her life she's been a medieval sword-fighting knight, mermaid trainer, Cosplayer, Irish step-dancer, Camogie Keeper, Health Coach, & Tech Consultant.

She learned at age 14 that she was intersex, motivating her to become an advocate for herself and learn to care for this human body she was given. Lacking resources on this subject, she spent many hours at an old computer trying to make sense of it. That is, until she built her own computer, which inspired a lifelong passion for technology.

She loves sharing her story to empower people to make informed healthcare decisions for themselves. While her roots started in doTERRA, sharing plant-based solutions with others, she now runs Nerd Marketing Agency for entrepreneurs & agencies to get their businesses systemized, automated, & online.

DEFYING BARRIERS

By Colleen McCartney

All throughout my life, my parents drilled into me that, living in Northern Virginia, I needed to find a job that made plenty of money. This was problematic, though, because I wasn't good at anything in school. I was drawn to technology school and excited to find that tech made sense to me—I just got it.

Because my brain understood tech so intuitively, I never understood how others struggled with it. I figured that anyone would be able to learn the same things just as quickly and "get it" just like I did. It took a long time for me to recognize that I had a unique skill set that set me apart.

After about a decade in IT (a lucrative but, for me, toxic environment), I switched gears and got into the wellness network marketing industry. (To hear more about that journey, check out my chapter in *She Rises: Unstoppable Women In Health & Wellness*.) Because of my background in IT, I leaned into technology to support my new business from day one.

I jumped right into using a high-level tech program notorious in the industry for being confusing to use. But it made sense to me, so I thought its nickname, "Confusionsoft," was just a funny colloquial term. I didn't really understand that many people legitimately struggled with it. I also didn't realize that most businesses were bringing in six figures before they jumped into this level of software. But I recognized the value of investing in a platform to help grow the infrastructure of my business.

Using this program, I created a robust email series where customers received communication about a specific product every week for an entire year. It was designed so that, no matter what, they received consistent attention and communication from me. The beautiful thing was that it was an automated series, so I could set it and forget it. With my ADHD, I struggle with object permanence—once I finish doing something, I kind of forget it exists. This email series allowed me to support and grow my relationship with my customers without battling executive dysfunction. And although I didn't realize it until much later, it was a cornerstone of my business because every customer got ongoing touchpoints and education from me.

When I ran into a traumatic experience in my business which demolished my income, dropping from $5k+ to $500/mo, it broke my spirit. I went to a place of fear-based decisions and tried to start minimizing my expenses without considering the impact it would have on my client base and discontinued using this platform. I tried to duct tape individual cheap tech programs together (which didn't work well) and ended up hopping from platform to platform thinking, "There has to be something better out there." All the while, my customers weren't getting the same attention they were used to, and my business began to stall. Seeing my decisions' impact on my clients and business partners, I recognized I needed to find a business coach.

Luckily I found someone who could see in me what I couldn't. Over the next few years, as she coached me to level up my skills and self-belief, I ended up doing a lot of tech work for her and her clients, and she pulled my genius out of me. She taught her customer follow-up process to her clients and paired it with existing software. As more people joined her program, more people needed my tech support. She kept referring more clients to me, so I was building an audience of online entrepreneurs, which was the seedling that would eventually grow into me creating and running my own digital marketing agency.

I started doing bigger tech projects for larger clients because I had a unique talent to walk into any system and figure it out. I was never scared that I couldn't solve a problem. My sheer audacity to expect technology to work and that I could find a solution meant I could walk into any platform and get projects done. Because these things seemed to just work and were easy for me to fix, I ended up undercharging people, not realizing how valuable my skills were.

I had my network marketing customers and a growing number of tech clients before I realized I needed to find a better solution to support my array of clientele. I'd been eyeing a new system for marketing agencies but was very intimidated because the belief in myself was just not there yet—*how can little ol' me run a marketing agency? I just do tech support and sell oils!* What I should have been telling myself was: *Figure out the first step and take it—don't worry about what comes after that.*

Throughout my life, ADHD has always been a challenge, yet somehow during this time, it became my superpower. You may not know this, but ADHD doesn't necessarily mean you are constantly distracted and struggle to focus on things (although that is definitely a part of it!). It also means you can be hyper-focused, and the amount of work I could crank out during a period of hyper-focus made me excellent at what I did. I'm that person who can start on a project at 8:00 PM when everyone else is offline, and without the constant distraction of other people who need my attention, I can work the entire night and make a ton of progress until the sun is starting to come up.

Cue Winter Solstice 2021. We were mid-pandemic, with businesses closing left and right. I could practically feel the cries of the healers who wanted to help people but were overwhelmed by tech. After many words of encouragement from my clients to start my own agency, I cried my way through the first steps of getting it up and running as I worked through my limiting beliefs. I worked feverishly night and day for ten days, and on New Year's Eve 2021, I launched my system for wellness professionals.

Since my audience was mainly wellness network marketers, that was the extent of my dream—it was all I let myself believe I could do. An agency to serve wellness network marketers WAS the dream. As I built the system for my company, I thought I could also replicate what I had created for other companies. The dream was slowly growing bigger. I was starting to dream bigger, but I would soon find out that I was still dreaming small.

It was a quick springboard from there to realize that other industries needed the tech solution I was providing my current clients. This idea was both exhilarating and crippling (darn you, anxiety!).

The first year with my marketing agency was a total roller coaster. I made a lot of decisions based on emotions rather than facts because I was moving at the speed of light and had no time to do anything but react. I went through several ups and downs throughout the process (and had a lot of all-nighters), going from feeling like I was on top of the world to questioning every business decision I'd ever made and being on the brink of quitting.

To combat this exhaustive back-and-forth state, I started Cognitive Behavioral Therapy. This helped me identify what the true thoughts and statements about me were and what was just my jerk inner self bullying me with lies. I learned that you must be the one who tells yourself what is true. You have to be the one that makes the decisions that navigate your life, your business, and anything you do. You have to be able to work through the fear. And when you are struggling in business, go look at your numbers. Numbers don't lie. Numbers don't have feelings. Numbers, not your feelings, will show you how your business is actually progressing.

I'm happy to report that while I know the journey to self-belief is far from over, my vision for my business and my future has expanded way beyond what I originally thought I was capable of doing. From being low-level tech support, afraid to charge $30 an hour for my time, I now run my own marketing agency, supporting over 60 small businesses. I'm turning my attention now to helping nurture other agencies and helping them to forge their own path. I'm using my zone of genius as a positive force to help as many other people out there as possible. None of this would have been possible if I hadn't ignored the voice in my head saying I wasn't enough and decided to take that first step forward.

Remember—If you have an idea or a vision for something you want to create, you are the only one who can decide what you are capable of.

Kelley Kaupas Rheault

Purple Camo Solutions
Founder/Owner/Success Coach

http://linkedin.com/in/kelley-kaupas-rheault-5705a31a
https://www.facebook.com/kelley.rheault
https://linktr.ee/PurpleCamo
Purple-Camo.com

Kelley is a Florida native that joined the Air Force after high school, serving 6 years as an Airborne German Linguist. After her enlistment, she earned her BA in Modern Languages with a focus on International Business, from Montana State University.

She created her own insurance agency primarily marketing LegalShield in 1997. In this role she works with large multinational companies, trains new agents, and speaks in front of numerous groups. She currently ranks as one of the top 20 associates worldwide.

In 2018, after receiving her life and business coaching certificate, she launched "The Transitioning Warrior", a Veteran's organization that supports military men and women in discovering their purpose and passion after the military.

Kelley is a proud mom to a teenage son, Austin, and is grateful to have had the opportunity to homeschool him for several years.

Her mission is to empower others to live their best life!

BEYOND THE MILLIONAIRES CLUB

By Kelley Kaupas Rheault

I feel so blessed to be surrounded by the beauty of the Maroon Bells, a gorgeous mountain range on the outskirts of Aspen. Being able to travel to exotic locations in the U.S. and abroad, visiting friends and family along the way, is one of the greatest gifts of being an entrepreneur, and running my own insurance agency with LegalShield. Work hard / play hard is my motto, and what's such an additional bonus, with this type of business, I can work from anywhere. During this trip, I truly combined work with pleasure because I opened up a new employee benefits group account in Aspen.

Speaking of LegalShield, my phone is ringing, and it's from our corporate office… let me get to a quiet place because they don't call very often, so when they do I always answer. To my amazement and surprise, I am informed that my commissions, since I started as an agent with LegalShield in 1997, have reached $1 million, and they are officially welcoming me as the newest member of the prestigious *Millionaires Club.*

WHOA… I'm breathless right now. So beyond excited! And I thought I was already on cloud nine being on this trip, now this call puts not just a cherry, but the entire cherry tree on top!

Some associates hit this milestone much quicker than I have, but as "they" say, it's not a sprint but a marathon, and comparisonitis is not a good practice in life. Easy to say, right? But actually, it's one of the hardest things to do. It's so easy to see someone else's success and wonder what's wrong with me—why don't I have that same success and those same income levels? I'm just as talented, and sometimes even more so.

This lesson was difficult for me to learn, and I continue to work on it every day—that we are on our personal journey, and so is everyone else.

We don't know their background, connections, work ethic, or circumstances, so we shouldn't compare to them. In my case, it only led to more self-doubt, negative self-talk, and a huge nudge to quit. Now I practice the belief that we are here to run our own race, stay in our lane, and the success will come if we DREAM BIG, WORK HARD and STAY CONSISTENT!

I choose to be grateful for my journey and the steep ups and downs. It's 2011, and it's been 14 years since I launched my business, but I have to admit I never expected to earn $1 million in this career.

I feel extremely blessed; I've had such an incredible lifestyle these past 14 years. My first and only goal was to make enough to pay my monthly expenses without needing to get a "real" job. I love the freedom of being an entrepreneur—the stress of the hustle not so much, but I love being my own boss and controlling my daily life decisions. I did dream big and took a leap of faith to become an entrepreneur and work for myself, but now I'm doing bigger because I've earned a significant living.

Five years have passed, and I'm cruising right along. I've been blessed to homeschool Austin; we travel about once a month and live in a beautiful, high-end complex in Boynton Beach.. So why am I feeling such a significant pull to do more? And why do I feel like such an imposter when I walk into the room to speak to and train new LegalShield associates, receiving such wonderful accolades? *If they only knew how little of my true potential I'm using, no one would ever clap for me and my new title as a millionaire club member.*

I can sum it up by saying; I was becoming very uncomfortable with my comfortable lifestyle and income level. I knew I could do more, and it was time I figured it out and pushed myself to do bigger.

When we throw these feelings out to the universe and ask these types of questions to ourselves, I truly believe the universe listens and conspires for us. My answer started with another life-changing call from one of my best friends and business colleagues, Thommy with an H. He sounded extremely nervous, abnormal for him, and he let me know that he was out in San Diego in the middle of his certification to become a life/business coach, and one of the last tasks he needed to do was reach out and find coaching clients. Thommy had no idea the thoughts that I had been having, the internal need to do more and to figure out how to grow my footprint in LegalShield and beyond. He was completely surprised when without hesitation, I said... *Yes, absolutely, I want to coach with you!*

Although I had lots of mentors, followed some great leaders, and attended every training and conference I could, I had never had an official one-on-one coach for myself, and it was a little frightening at first. I was definitely not comfortable opening up to anyone like this.

Working with Thommy and participating in some other Life on Fire events opened my eyes beyond anything I could have imagined. At the end of a week-long bootcamp, I again shocked myself by committing to their 6-month coaching program and becoming certified. I couldn't think about a $10,000 investment, which at the time, I had no idea where it was going to come from. Still, my belief was so strong that there was really no other answer than "yes."

It is so important that we follow our heart and intuition, and as I've heard it said... take a leap of faith, and our wings will appear on the way down.

Toward the end of our six months together for the certification, we had an in-person event in San Diego. Sitting in one of our small group sessions with our facilitator, it seemed very strange when he asked, "What pisses you off?"

How will this question lead us to find our niche within our own coaching business? Well, I participated, and another big surprise came up for me. *It pisses me off that as veterans, we go off and serve our country, and when we come back to step into civilian careers, most end up settling for jobs that are way below our pay grade and way below what experience and expertise we are bringing to the table.*

It was strange that this was what was screaming so loudly in my head. Although I went to the VA as my medical provider due to a service-connected disability, I never really identified as a veteran in other ways. But the lightbulb undoubtedly went off. I wanted to coach veterans for free and pass on the incredible knowledge I had gained by running my own successful business for almost 20 years, becoming an entrepreneur able to earn over six figures from home.

About a year later, in 2018, my website was complete, and I was launching "The Transitioning Warrior." I came up with this name during a meditation session in Sante Fe, meditating with one of my best friends and spiritual mentors, Jana Fleming. I dreamed big and became an entrepreneur, but I did bigger by creating an organization as my passion project to give back to my veteran community.

It is so important to have big dreams in our lives, but you might be surprised when those initial dreams are vastly exceeded because our internal drive and spirit lead us to something much bigger!

GIVING HONOR TO WHOM HONOR IS DUE.

UNITED STATES OF AMERICA
UNITED STATES AIR FORCE
MCMXLVII

SERVICE: 1985-1990

AIM HIGH. DREAM BIG ALWAYS WORK HARD AND NEVER FORGET TO PLAY HARD, TOO!

KELLEY RHEAULT

Kara Long

The Memory Collective
Founder and Memory Archivist

https://www.linkedin.com/in/karalong/
https://www.facebook.com/karalongstories
https://www.instagram.com/tmcstory/
www.thememorycollectiveco.com
www.thememorycollectiveco.com/starter-guide

Kara Long is a writer, artist, and musician gone entrepreneur, born in the little historical town of Irvington, Indiana. In her childhood, she experienced several losses of close family members that shaped her future life and interests. Her lifelong passion for writing, music, and art followed her into college, where she studied Music Technology and Media Arts. After graduating, she knew she wanted to do something big and give back to the world in a big way with her skills, talents, and experiences, but wasn't sure how. When the idea of The Memory Collective came to her in early 2019, she realized her whole life had been preparing her for this huge mission. Now, she helps aging parents capture their legacy through recorded oral storytelling, so they can preserve their memories, heritage, and connections to their loved ones forever.

DREAMS AND LEGACIES

By Kara Long

In my line of work, we spend a lot of time talking about childhood and its key memories. I could write an entire book about my childhood experience, despite having forgotten a lot of it. It was a happy time for me that became all the more precious because it ended abruptly when I was 12.

From the time I was a kid, I dreamed of becoming something truly great—something memorable, badass, and impactful. I was going to be a world-famous, best-selling author, a showcased artist in multiple mediums, a multi-instrumentalist rockstar, a world-renowned treasure hunter like Indiana Jones, and a world-saving superhero for good measure. My childhood was spent blissfully lost in imagination—writing epic stories, sketching and sculpting and building my ideas, singing to an invisible crowd of raving fans, hunting for ancient artifacts and treasure in the attic, and saving the day with magical powers to defeat the imaginary bad guy.

The catalyst for all these dreams and daydreams was, undoubtedly, my family. As an only child on my dad's side, I spent a lot of time with my Grandma Florence, my dad, and my aunts and uncles. Dad, who was a science teacher, writer, photographer, marathon runner, music enthusiast, and general outdoorsman, encouraged my creativity and education. He and I would sit out on our front porch during thunderstorms, and he'd teach me about the relationship between thunder and lightning and make up stories about camping adventures. Aunt Pat, who was my childhood hero, taught me to draw and write and be patient and compassionate. My mom was an animal-loving could-have-gone-professional-clarinetist-turned-network-engineer who read to me almost every day. My stepdad, Bob, was a wizard on the keyboard, and his son, Brian, was a badass rock drummer. No matter who I talked to in my family, I was shown the values of kindness, patience, doing the right thing, and learning. They all supported me in fulfilling my dreams, and I'm well aware how lucky I was to have it.

But as I said before, my childhood ended at 12 years old. That was when we got the news that my big brother, Brian, drowned. He was twenty-four. It was unthinkable–and my first experience with the crushing weight of death and grief.

Then Dad started getting weaker and weaker. I knew something was wrong, and I knew now that people could die and what it felt like to lose someone. Just before my thirteenth birthday, Dad went in for a biopsy. His heart failed, and he went into a coma. Meanwhile, Aunt Pat was diagnosed with Stage four breast cancer. Dad died four months after the biopsy, after a rollercoaster of recoveries and resuscitations. Aunt Pat deteriorated over the next nine years as the chemo fogged her mind, body, and spirit. Grandma Florence passed when I was 17, Aunt Pat when I was 21, and my Grandma Jo and Grandpa John when I was 25.

I was lost for a while. Writing and music were my crutches, but as I attempted to identify and plan my future through and after high school, I was plagued with depression, anxiety, indecision, and grief. I didn't know what I wanted to do with my life other than the massive dreams that felt unreachable. And, though none of those dreams were forgotten, new perspectives on life, loss, and what was important shaped me. I thought about becoming an architect, inspired by what Brian studied, or psychology to help others with grief and anxiety, or teaching like Dad and Aunt Pat. I wanted to follow my dreams but didn't know how to become whatever "being an artist" even looked like. The one thing that remained was wanting to make an impact on the world in some way—to give back, to solve a big problem, to make everyone I'd lost (and everyone I hadn't) proud of me and honor their legacy.

It was sometime in college when I started to finally take inventory of what memories I had of everyone I'd lost. I'd expected to be able to list them off like a roll call. They hadn't happened that long ago, relatively speaking. But I couldn't. There were obvious gaps and gaping holes in my memories. Dad and I had gone camping it seemed like hundreds of times. So why could I only remember a few distinct memories? Then I realized I only had one memory left of my brother—but it was just a hodgepodge of several fragments of memories on different occasions. The stories Grandma Jo told me about her childhood after she and her parents moved from Italy—the stories I'd thought, "Wow! These are *great* stories. I never knew this about her!"—were also forgotten. Why hadn't my brain flagged these memories as being worth keeping? Didn't it realize these memories were all that connected me to the people I'd loved and lost?

In 2019, all the experiences, losses, realizations, skills, and connections aligned into an idea that profoundly changed the course of my life. The idea was: helping people explore, tell, and record their life stories aloud, so that no matter what happened, their family could always see them, hear their voices, remember those stories, and connect back to the person they loved. It felt like a weight had been lifted off my shoulders. This was what life prepared me to do. From the childhood attic searches for ancient artifacts to the emphasis on storytelling and crippling loss, it felt like I'd been divinely set up to do this. In a matter of days, I went from someone with exactly zero business experience, who had virtually no idea what she wanted to do with her life, to an entrepreneur with a focused mission to help preserve and save people's family treasures all around the world.

This dream was 29 years in the making. The Memory Collective was founded on the eight-year anniversary of Aunt Pat's death. And the more I began to explore the concept and reflect on the impact it could have had on *my* life, the more the mission began to take shape. If The

Memory Collective existed when Dad and Aunt Pat knew they were sick and if this service were a household name they'd known about, I'd like to think they would have used it. I could have had my dad's voice—which I haven't heard in 19 years—telling stories about his childhood, high school, college, and me. I realized that if *I* used a service like The Memory Collective a couple years after Brian and Dad passed, that I wouldn't have those gaping holes in my memory. If I'd recorded Aunt Pat telling her life story before the chemo fogged her brain, or if I'd recorded Grandma Jo telling me those stories of her parents from Italy, I would still have them. If I start recording my own life stories right now, there will be no limit to what could be recalled later in life. And if I have kids and something happens to me while they are still young, they will know exactly who their mother was.

Beyond that—think of the impact on individuals with Alzheimer's and their families. I recently had a client tell me that playing back the videos for his aunt with Alzheimer's helped her become temporarily lucid. Recorded Oral Storytelling is so much more powerful than people realize.

That's the biggest problem I see people facing. Most people have no idea how priceless those recorded stories would be until it's too late. It takes a tragedy for them to fully understand. That's why a large part of my mission involves raising awareness about Recorded Oral Storytelling and educating people about the power of this ancient craft. While my first goal is to reach those most at risk of memory loss, sickness, or death, one of the most beautiful realizations I've had is that this service is perfect for all ages, walks of life, and situations. Any memory someone has and wants to keep—for themselves, for children, descendants, or even just for posterity—can be. Memories of childhood, family, relationships, weddings, military service, careers, struggles and triumphs, team sports, family vacations, pets, crafts and creations, philosophies, beliefs, and affirmations—all these and countless more topics make up the most rewarding part of my job. It's a privilege to see the beauty of humanity through their stories, and know these people will live on forever, cherished by their families for all time.

My big dream? To see The Memory Collective reach families across the globe in every spoken and signed language, to make loss easier to bear, and to be a household name. I have a lifetime of experience dreaming big thanks to the influence of my family. And with a network of people spreading the word about The Memory Collective, joining the mission, and encouraging loved ones to record their stories, we can do bigger *faster*, and reach people before it is too late.

If you'd like to learn more about The Memory Collective, Recorded Oral Storytelling, and our mission, please visit www.TheMemory CollectiveCo.com and reach out to me directly at info@TheMemory CollectiveCo.com.

Jenna Leigh

President of Provenance Consulting Group

https://www.linkedin.com/in/jennaschwartz1/
https://www.facebook.com/jenna.schwartz.58?mibextid=LQQJ4d
https://instagram.com/jenna.leigh.s?igshid=YmMyMTA2M2Y=
https://web3pcg.com/
https://www.stoneridgepartners.com/

Jenna Leigh is a master connector, who uses her ability to bring together like-minded individuals, create countless deals, and deep relationships. As co-director for Tampa's Boss Talks, Jenna leads and moderates events with intent to empower and mentor attendees. Jenna prides herself on giving back, leading her to co-found Work for Peace, a charity that aims to increase awareness of Domestic Violence and aid those impacted by it. Outside of her personal endeavors, Jenna is a force in the business world as a founding member of the Provenance Consulting Group, an executive coaching and consulting firm, CGO for the burgeoning NFT Project "Pineapples in Paradise," and Buy-side associate partner for the M&A Advisory firm, Stoneridge Partners. Jenna's background also includes a decade of Health IT experience, sales and marketing. With a passion for bringing value and positively impacting those around her, Jenna captivates & encourages her audience to take action.

FACT OR MYTH: YOU CAN BE WHATEVER YOUR HEART DESIRES

By Jenna Leigh

Growing up we are often asked, "what do you want to be when you grow up?" As children, "we are able to respond with what speaks to our heart without the consequences of reality. Whether it is to be an astronaut, fire fighter, doctor, or more there is little to no thought about how," as an astronaut I'd be away from my family and live in extreme environments, or as a fire fighter the risk to my life and capped earning potential, or as a doctor the several years of schooling placing challenges on having a personal life. As an adult our desires come with a slap in the face of reality.

As a business coach, my partner Josh Hibbert, and I work with entrepreneurs, visionaries, and employees looking to build a path to their goals. For this chapter, I'd like to focus on the client who wants more out of their professional life and faces indecisiveness, using techniques we have used for years.

As many highschoolers do, I began evaluating my post-graduation options. For many this is one the first opportunities to decide what to do with our own lives and facing unchartered territory. Thoughts might look like, do I go to college, trade school, military, gap year, travel, etc.? I used an early variation of a process that our consulting firm now calls the PCG Decision Making Process. [1] The process was born from my need and tailored to support others too.

As humans, we tend to operate on emotion and use logic to reason with ourselves. The PCG Decision Making Process takes advantage of this and helps us understand our options, organize our thoughts, and offers logical decision-making solutions that still take our emotions into account.

Step 1: Determine what type of decision you want to make.

For this chapter we will use a professional change decision that needs to be made.

The first step we like to take is [2], what does "more" mean to you? Examples we often hear are

- I want to make more money
- I want more flexibility in my schedule (work-life balance)
- I want to feel fulfilled

…and let's be real… this sounds like almost all of us, right?

For my highschool process this looked like "I want to be able to get a good a job." A very general desire.

There isn't much that would allow us to make a clear decision with the above list, so where do we move next?

Step 2: List your options.

Let's discussing what our options are, examples can include:

- Staying in a current position
- Applying for a new job—Position X at Company Y
- Beginning my own business—Create a company that solves for A
- Going back to *school* (professional/technical/credentialing) - Going to school for B so I can move into profession C

If you are reading this and going: "but I don't know what the h**l I want to do," there is nothing wrong with you! There are techniques we work through with our clients to get there that will require a deeper dive. For the purpose of today, it is critical to be specific on the available options before going to the next step.

In my personal experience using this method in high school, my only logical choice was college, yet I had no idea which school to go to and was overwhelmed with the abundance of schools to apply to. My options looked like a handful of schools I had an interest in.

Step 3: List your priorities, wants, and non-negotiables.

Grab a piece of paper or excel spreadsheet and, along the left-hand side, list off each of your thoughts as a common category such as:

- Earning potential
- Stability
- Work-life balance
- Company culture

For me, I slowly started to pick factors that mattered to me, the first was wanting a small to mid-size school since, in true entrepreneurial form, I knew there would be no shot I could pay attention in a large lecture hall.

From there, I realized this one general factor was not nearly enough. Fortunately, I had the privilege of supportive parents who took me locally and to a few out-of-state schools to tour. This due diligence allowed several new factors of what I liked and didn't like to begin presenting themselves. [5]

Having a deep understanding of your options is pertinent, as it will present your unique wants. [remember if there is something that would make you unhappy include this too—catch the one at the end below ;)]:

- Can bring my dog to work
- They have a complimentary barista and chef for breakfast
- It's my dream
- I'm the owner
- I like the status of this option
- The office smells like fish

Now we can really get through your emotions and logic! Take out a piece of paper or use a spreadsheet. On the top row list your options from Step 2. Then, along the left-hand side, begin listing each category/thought from this step (3).

Here is how my Step 3 process went. I took a yellow legal pad, and on the far left-hand side I began writing each factor line by line: internship opportunities, weather, cost, cheerleading team to try out for, ease of getting home, and so on until I had over 25 factors that affected my opinion of each school. [6]

Step 4: Rate your options logically

On your piece of paper or spreadsheet go ahead and rate all of your categories 1-5—one being the worst and five being the best. At the bottom, total your scores. This allows us to organize thoughts logically on a macro level.

	School 1 - In FL	School 2 - In Iowa
Weather	5	1
Internship opportunities	5	4
Cheerleading team to tryout for	0	5
Total	10	10

Like you see in the chart above, my experience resulted in both schools I was looking at receiving the exact same score of 94...[7] *"Goodness, now what do I do?" I thought to myself!*

Step 5: Rate your options emotionally

Take a look at your list, and based on the number of categories, circle the factors that would make you the happiest and the ones that would make you the most unhappy. From there, go ahead and retotal your options (do not change your 1-5 rankings), but also total those emotional rankings. Use the chart below to determine how many categories to circle.

	What makes you most happy	What would make you most unhappy
Under 10 categories	2	1
11-20 categories	3	2
21 + categories	3	3

In my experience, It occurred to me that I was ranking trying out for a cheerleading team as the same rating as internship opportunities when one of these was way more important to me than the other. Once I chose the factors most important to me and the factor that would make me the least happy, the two schools were no longer a tie; it became strikingly clear which school to attend.[8]

Due to only showing a fraction of my categories, I am selecting just two, as you can see below.

	School 1 - FL	School 2 - Iowa
Weather	5	1
Internship opportunities	5	4
Total	**10**	**5**

While I was voted 'most likely to cheer in college,' and it was something I really wanted to do, this method forced me to choose what meant most to me. I grew up 45 minutes North of Chicago—I was DONE with the cold, and I really wanted to work at an internship during the semester.

One of the most common fears we have as humans is fear of change or the unknown, so moving forward and taking action on a decision can be challenging. I hope this method allows you to marry your desires and logic as you come across indecisiveness.

Does this answer whether "you can be whatever your heart desires" is a fact or a myth? I'm curious to hear your thoughts!

JOIN THE MOVEMENT!
#BAUW

Becoming An Unstoppable Woman
With She Rises Studios

She Rises Studios was founded by Hanna Olivas and Adriana Luna Carlos, the mother-daughter duo, in mid-2020 as they saw a need to help empower women around the world. They are the podcast hosts of the *She Rises Studios Podcast* as well as Amazon best-selling authors and motivational speakers who travel the world. Hanna and Adriana are the movement creators of #BAUW - Becoming An Unstoppable Woman: The movement has been created to universally impact women of all ages, at whatever stage of life, to overcome insecurities, and adversities, and develop an unstoppable mindset. She Rises Studios educates, celebrates, and empowers women globally.

Looking to Join Us in our Next Anthology
or Publish YOUR Own?

She Rises Studios Publishing offers full-service publishing, marketing, book tour, and campaign services. For more information, contact info@sherisesstudios.com

We are always looking for women who want to share their stories and expertise and feature their businesses on our podcasts, in our books, and in our magazines.

SEE WHAT WE DO

OUR PODCAST   **OUR BOOKS**   **OUR SERVICES**

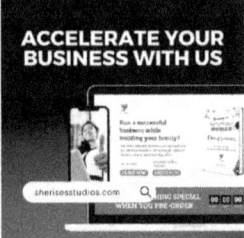

Be featured in the Becoming An Unstoppable Woman magazine, published in 13 countries and sold in all major retailers. Get the visibility you need to LEVEL UP in your business!

Have your own TV show streamed across major platforms like Roku TV, Amazon Fire Stick, Apple TV and more!

Learn to leverage your expertise. Build your online presence and grow your audience with Fenix TV.
https://fenixtv.sherisesstudios.com/

Visit www.SheRisesStudios.com to see how YOU can join the #BAUW movement and help your community to achieve the UNSTOPPABLE mindset.

Have you checked out the *She Rises Studios Podcast?*

Find us on all MAJOR platforms: Spotify, IHeartRadio, Apple Podcasts, Google Podcasts, etc.

Looking to become a sponsor or build a partnership?

Email us at info@sherisesstudios.com